Dragonwings

and Related Readings

McDougal Littell
A HOUGHTON MIFFLIN COMPANY

Evanston, Illinois   Boston   Dallas

Acknowledgments

Don Congdon Associates, Inc.: "The Flying Machine" from *Golden Apples of the Sun* by Ray Bradbury; Copyright 1953, renewed, © 1981 by Ray Bradbury. Reprinted by permission of Don Congdon Associates, Inc.

Beverly McLoughland: "Crazy Boys" by Beverly McLoughland from *Hand in Hand: An American History Through Poetry*, edited by Lee Bennett Hopkins, Copyright © 1994. Reprinted by permission of the author.

Literary Estate of Joseph Colin Murphey: "The Skydivers" by Joseph Colin Murphey from *Quartet: A Magazine of the Arts*. Reprinted by permission of Dave Oliphant, executor for the Literary Estate of Joseph Colin Murphey.

Forbes, Inc.: "The Chinese Must Go" by Bernard A. Weisberger from *American Heritage* magazine; Copyright © 1993 by Forbes Inc. Reprinted by permission of American Heritage Magazine, a division of Forbes, Inc.

Simon & Schuster Inc.: "Ginger for the Heart" from *Tales from Gold Mountain* by Paul Yee; Copyright © 1989 by Paul Yee. Reprinted with the permission of Simon & Schuster Books for Young Readers, an imprint of Simon & Schuster Children's Publishing Division.

Dragonwings Copyright © 1975 by Laurence Yep. Reprinted by permission of HarperCollins Publishers.

Illustration by Ronald Himler, Copyright © 1995 HarperCollins Publishers.
Background (below): Copyright © Bill Pogue.
Author photo: K. Yep.

ISBN 0-395-77136-6
2002 Impression.

10 11 12 13 14 15 – DCI – 07 06 05

Contents

Continued

Dragonwings

Laurence Yep

Chapter 1

The Land of the Demons
(February–March 1903)

Ever since I can remember, I had wanted to know about the Land of the Golden Mountain, but my mother had never wanted to talk about it. All I knew was that a few months before I was born, my father had left our home in the Middle Kingdom, or *China,* as the white demons call it, and traveled over the sea to work in the demon land. There was plenty of money to be made among the demons, but it was also dangerous. My own grandfather had been lynched about thirty years before by a mob of white demons almost the moment he had set foot on their shores.

Mother usually said she was too busy to answer my questions. It was a fact that she was overworked, for Grandmother was too old to help her with the heavy work, and she had to try to do both her own work and Father's on our small farm. The rice had to be grown from seeds, and the seedlings transplanted to the paddies, and the paddies tended and harvested. Besides this, she always had to keep one eye on our very active pig to keep him from rooting in our small vegetable patch. She also had to watch our three chickens, who loved to wander away from our farm.

Any time I brought up the subject of the Golden Mountain, Mother suddenly found something going wrong on our farm. Maybe some seedlings had not been planted into their underwater beds properly, or perhaps our pig was eating the wrong kind of garbage, or maybe one of our chickens was dirtying our doorway. She always had some good excuse for not talking about the Golden Mountain. I knew she was afraid of the place, because every chance we got, she would take me into the small temple in our village and we would pray for Father's safety, though she would never tell me what she was afraid of. It was a small satisfaction to her that our prayers had worked so far. Mother was never stingy about burning incense for Father.

I was curious about the Land of the Golden Mountain mainly because my father was there. I had, of course, never seen my father. And we could not go to live with him for two reasons. For one thing, the white demons would not let wives join their husbands on the Golden Mountain because they did not want us settling there permanently. And for another thing, our own clans discouraged wives from leaving because it would mean an end to the money the husbands sent home to their families—money which was then spent in the Middle Kingdom. The result was that the wives stayed in the villages, seeing their husbands every five years or so if they were lucky—though sometimes there were longer separations, as with Mother and Father.

We had heavy debts to pay off, including the cost of Father's ticket. And Mother and Grandmother had decided to invest the money Father sent to us in buying more land and livestock. At any rate, there was no money to spare for Father's visit back home. But my mother never complained about the hard work or the loneliness. As she said, we were the people of the Tang, by which she meant we were a tough, hardy, patient race. (We did not call ourselves *Chinese,* but the people of the Tang, after that famous dynasty that had helped settle our area some eleven hundred years ago. It would be the same as if an *English* demon called himself a man of the *Tudors,* the dynasty of *Henry VIII* and of *Elizabeth I*—though demon names sound so drab compared to ours.)

But sometimes Mother's patience wore thin. It usually happened when we walked over to the small side room in the Temple, where classes were also held. Like many other people, Mother and Grandmother could neither read nor write; but for a small fee, the village schoolmaster would read one of Father's weekly letters to us or write a letter at our dictation. In the evening after dinner, we would join the line of people who had a husband or brothers or sons overseas. There we would wait until it was our turn to go inside the Temple, and Mother would nervously turn the letter over and over again in her hands until Grandmother would tell her she was going to wear out the letter before we could read it.

To tell the truth, I knew as little about my father as I knew about the Land of the Golden Mountain. But Mother made sure that I knew at least one important thing about him: He was a maker of the most marvelous kites. Everyone in the village said he was a master of his craft, and his kites were often treasured by their owners like family heirlooms. As soon as I was big enough to hold the string, Mother took me out to the hill near our village where we could fly one of Father's kites. Just the two of us would go.

But you won't appreciate my father's skill if you think flying a kite—any kind of a kite—is just putting a bunch of paper and sticks up into the air. I remember the first time we went to fly a kite. There was nothing like the thrill when my kite first leaped up out of Mother's hands into the air. Then she showed me how to pull and tug and guide the kite into the winds. And when the winds caught the kite, it shot upward. She told me then how the string in my hand was like a leash and the kite was like a hound that I had sent hunting, to flush a sunbeam or a stray phoenix out of the clouds.

But then she warned me that I had to stay alert, because sometimes the winds would try to tear the kite from my hand and I would have to hold on; or maybe the winds would try to drop my kite so it would smash to the ground. In that case, I would have to hurry up and reel in the slack and pull and steer the kite back into the winds until, just to get rid of the nuisance, the winds would take my kite where I wanted it to go.

I failed miserably the first times I tried to fly the kite, but Mother would not let me give up; and eventually I got quick enough and strong enough and smart enough so that my kite would be flying far overhead—so far away that I would lose sight of the string I had attached to the kite, and the kite would seem to be some colored patch of rainbow that was following me about. And then Mother would say that she was sure the kite was flying so high that the Jade Emperor, the Lord of Heaven and Earth, could admire my kite from his palace window. That was what flying a kite was all about.

And of course, Father's kites were the most truly

balanced and the strongest and yet the most beautiful. In fact, his kites practically flew themselves. At first Mother only let me use Father's ordinary kites. He had made some special kites just before he left, when he knew my mother was pregnant; but Mother said I could not fly those kites until I was older and wiser—that is, when I turned eight. (The Tang people count the first nine months the mother carries the baby as the baby's first year. By demon reckoning, I was only seven.) I can't say who was prouder, my mother or I, when I finally managed to fly Father's special kites.

One was a sharply climbing swallow kite that was hard to get up, but there was nothing as fast as the swallow once it was up. The swallow swooped down with the slightest flick of the wrist or soared skyward with the tiniest jerk of the string. There was a large, long caterpillar kite, too, that took even longer to get up than the swallow, but once it was in the sky, it would stay forever, crawling back and forth over the clouds.

But the best thing about flying any of the kites was what it did for Mother. She would throw off all her cares and become young again, running with me or taking a turn at flying the kite. She would chatter on about the things that she and Father used to do when they were young, for they had both grown up here. She taught me everything that Father had ever shown her about flying kites. She said that one of the first things he would want to see when he returned home for a visit was how well I could fly them. But even at these moments, Mother would never speak of the Golden Mountain.

But I felt that since I was now eight and had mastered the hardest of Father's kites to fly, I was also old enough to get some answers. Mother still would not talk about the Golden Mountain, and in fact got mad at me. Grandmother felt sorry for me then, and she tried to tell me, among other things, why we called *America* the Land of the Golden Mountain. "It's because there's a big mountain there," she said. "The mountain's a thousand miles high and three thousand miles wide, and all a man has to do is wait until the sun warms the mountain and then scoop the gold into big buckets."

I squirmed on the bench. "Then why doesn't Father go get the gold instead of washing clothes?"

Grandmother shook her head. "It's because of the demons, you see. They roam the mountain up and down, and they beat up any of our men who try to get the gold. The demons use clubs as big as trees, and they kick them and do worse things. But if you do the work they tell you to do, then they let you take a little pinch of gold."

"Is that what happened to Grandfather? Did the demons catch him when he was trying to sneak some of the gold into his pockets?"

Grandmother sighed. She had been married to Grandfather only a year before he had left to make his fortune. "Perhaps, but," she added meaningfully, "the demons would just as soon beat up the Tang people for no good reason."

I nodded in understanding when Grandmother spoke of senseless beatings, for I had seen some of the other "guests" who had returned. There was Crook Arm, whose left arm dangled down uselessly by his side with two of his fingers missing. And there were other men whose backs were stooped, their fingers gnarled and their faces worn and tired as old masks (I did not know at the time that this was simply all from a life of hard work; I thought that torture had done this to them). Many of them had the lung disease—*tuberculosis* was the demon word—and they hacked and spat constantly. Bit by bit they coughed up their broken lungs. Everyone in the village knew they had not long to live. Still more returned in their coffins, a silent testimony to the harshness of their demon "hosts."

I did not realize that I would find out at first hand about the Golden Mountain. One day, shortly after my ninth birthday (or eighth, as the demons count such things) we had a visitor, our cousin Hand Clap. He was in his fifties and lively as a cricket. He was a cousin because we had the same family name of Lee, though we had never seen him before. He said he had worked in the same store with my father and Uncle Bright Star overseas. Hand Clap obviously enjoyed the respect we gave him. Over tea, he told us he had decided to go back to the Land of the Golden Mountain and work a few more years while he still could. As he said, his two unmarried daughters were so ugly that they needed big dowries. But we knew he was going back for another reason.

Things had not remained the same in his village as he remembered them. You would say something about a family or a village in the district, and he would say that was nothing and compare it to something bigger or better that he had seen in his youth. The silk was finer, the air cleaner, the rice sweeter, the fields more fertile, the girls prettier, the boys stronger when he was a young man. And then, too, when he spoke of his home life, he said there were too many women around and too much fussing. Though he had been married since he was sixteen, he had spent nearly thirty years of his marriage apart from his wife. On the other hand, his face lit up whenever he spoke of the good things about living on the Golden Mountain—for the Tang people had learned to have their own good times there.

Mother, of course, asked Hand Clap to take a small gift over to Father.

"I think I've come for a much bigger gift," he said, and handed us a letter from my father. "Make sure that it's your husband's hand," he said.

Mother nodded. Grandmother grunted that it was her son's writing all right. Then Hand Clap picked up the letter and began to read it.

In his letter, my father said that he and Uncle Bright Star thought it was time for me to cross the sea. I don't remember too much of what happened after that. I think that Mother said I was too young and Grandmother shouted that she had already lost a husband to the demons. Then her son had left her, and now she was about to lose her only grandson. Through all of this, Hand Clap sat unperturbed.

I sat bolt upright in my chair as Hand Clap spoke. "His father wants him to come over now with me. He'll learn the demon tongue better when he's young."

"But the demons will beat Moon Shadow," Mother protested.

"They don't do that so much anymore." Hand Clap carefully wiped his sticky fingers on his tunic sleeve. "And they wouldn't do it to a child. Even the demons have some principles."

Grandmother leaned forward on her cane. "And what if there are some lawless ones? They might not know any better and beat him."

"Not while I and the Company are around," Hand Clap said. "And there are always the fighting brotherhoods."

"Big talk," Grandmother grunted. "You're like the blind man who catches sparrows and calls them phoenixes."

"And besides," Mother insisted, "Shadow doesn't want to go yet."

It was an important moment in my life. Perhaps the most important. I had never seen my father, though I had often tried to picture him from Mother's and Grandmother's descriptions of him. His letters were certainly warm enough, filled with his worries about us and his longing to be back home. But a man cannot be a father in a letter.

Mother had talked quite a bit about him and so had Grandmother; but that too was not the same. They were speaking about a young man who had lived in the Middle Kingdom, not a man who had endured the hardships and loneliness of living in the demon land. I knew he made kites; but as marvelous as his kites were, he and I could not spend the rest of our lives flying kites. I was afraid of the Golden Mountain, and yet my father, who lived there, wanted me to join him. I only knew that there was a certain rightness in life—the feeling you got when you did something the way you knew you should. I owed it to Father to obey him in everything—even if it meant going to such a fearful place as the Golden Mountain. And really, how really frightening could it be if Hand Clap wanted to go back? I turned to Mother and Grandmother. "I want to go," I said.

And that was that. I won't go through the tearful goodbyes, or the boat ride on the river to Canton, the port city, or the first few days on the demon boat. I was young and I was homesick and I was frightened—especially of all the sailors, for they were so tall and big and hairy I thought that they were tiger demons—special tigers with magical powers. Perhaps I should explain here that the Tang word for demon can mean many kinds of supernatural beings. A demon can be the ghost of a dead person, but he can also be a supernatural creature who can use his great powers for good as well as for evil, just like the dragons. It is much trickier to deal with a demon of the Middle Kingdom than an *American devil,* because you always know that the *American devil* means you harm.

I was frightened, and Hand Clap did nothing to ease my fear. One fellow passenger remembered a story about demon sailors who had fattened up their Tang passengers. The Tang people had thought it was a good deal till they were marched off the boat into a butcher's shop. And then Hand Clap said that was nothing, and went on to talk about a ship of tiger demons who plied their trade between Canton and Hell, delivering the Tang men for work there. Hand Clap cared little about the truth, and loved to let his imagination run wild. He told us about how the sailors had slept upside down on top of their heads with knives between their teeth, and so on.

So I could not understand his excitement when we neared the land of the demons. To my disappointment, I only saw a brown smudge on the horizon—as the Middle Kingdom had looked from a distance. There was no glittering mound of gold to be seen. And then Hand Clap took me below to the hold to rehearse my story for the customs demons. It was the one bit of practical advice I ever got from Hand Clap. When I came to the customs demons, I was to say I was eight, in the demon fashion, instead of nine as I truly was. I was to use my name in the wrong order, putting my family name after my personal name as the demons did. Otherwise the demons would write down the last word they heard, so that I would be called *Mister* Shadow instead of

Mister Lee. If I made any of those mistakes, I might not be allowed to land as the son of my father.

There was reason to worry, too, for just a few years ago, the demons had broken their own laws and turned away over twenty thousand of their former guests who had expected to be readmitted. This figure does not even reflect the large number of Tang men who could not get into the country for the first time. The demons, it seemed, were determined to cut down on the number of Tang people living on the Golden Mountain.

The demons kept us locked inside a long, two-story warehouse for a week before it was our turn to be questioned. I don't like to think about it too much. We were kept on the bottom story, where we slept and ate off the floors. All the time, we smelled the sewage and the bilge of the bay—besides which there was no way to bathe there, so after the long boat voyage, we were rather a fragrant group on our own.

Finally, though, when the demons called me for questioning, I found they already had a big bunch of papers on my father. Inside it was the record of his first interview, which ran for some one hundred and fifty pages. They spent an hour looking at it and then asking me questions about my village and kinsmen. They tried to trip me up so they could prove I was not my father's son, but they did not succeed.

Finally even the demons had to admit that I was who I claimed to be. Then they made me strip naked and took my measurements and poked me all around, and they wrote down all that information on a sheet of paper so that if I ever left their country, no one could sneak back in my place. They put that sheet into a new bunch of papers, which were on me. They also added the notes of our interview to that pile.

I only got my first close look at the land of the

Golden Mountain when Hand Clap and I were finally released and we stood together before the open doorway leading out of the warehouse where all the immigrants were taken. I saw plenty of hills, but not one golden one. And all the demon houses looked so strange. They were boxlike in shape, with no courtyards inside them, as if the demons hated fresh air but liked being shut up in something like a trunk. The houses had almost no ornamentation and were painted in dull colors—when they were painted at all. The little boxlike houses seemed so drab to me that I even felt sorry for the demons who lived in them, for they lived like prisoners without knowing they were in a prison.

Hand Clap had already sent word to Father by a friend who had been ahead of us in line and who had been released the day before, so we knew Father and the others would be waiting. I saw all the Tang men standing at the foot of the pier before the warehouse. I clutched my wooden box to my chest. It was about the length of my arm and about a third that in width; and it had a cunning metal clasp with a ring at the end. I would hook my finger into the ring and pull it up and the lid would open almost noiselessly. This was for my valuables. I played with the catch now nervously, studying the men.

They were all dressed alike, in either denim jackets or the big, black loose cotton tunics that reached to their hips and had wide, winglike sleeves. They also wore heavy blue demon trousers of denim. Some of them wore the cotton slipperlike shoes of the Tang men, while others wore demon boots. They all wore demon hats, with the crowns pushed up full and high and the brims down flat. I found myself wondering which of them were really Tang men and which might be demons in disguise.

Hand Clap waved toward one knot of men. "That's Uncle Bright Star." Hand Clap pointed at a fat, old man. He pointed out the rest of our Company. I heard him say that they must not have brought the wagon because of the crowds down here and the long wait for us. "And that tall man there," Hand Clap finished, looking at me, "that's your father."

I started to run. The others said hello as I went past them but I ignored them. I held my box so tightly against my chest that it hurt to breathe. Then I looked up at the tall man who stood over me. He was nearly five foot eight, which was tall for a Tang man in those days. He had a long, sharp face with almost elfin eyes.

He was my father and yet he was a stranger to me. I had never seen him.

I thought to myself, How can we ever speak to one another? He's as strange to me as a demon.

And then my father smiled. "Hello, boy," he said. He knelt down on the pier and held out his arms. "I've waited a long time to do this. Too long."

And I dropped my box and ran into his arms. I had arrived.

Chapter **2**

The Company
(April, 1903)

"So this is your boy," Uncle Bright Star said.

"Yes, Uncle." Father pushed me forward.

Uncle studied me as he would a new flatiron, looking for flaws. I stared back at him. They don't make men like Uncle Bright Star anymore. His hands were calloused by mining the *California* streams for gold, and his left index finger was twisted slightly from an accident when he had been helping to dig tunnels through the mountains for the railroad. Uncle had few "classmates" left. Classmates was the term which one government official might use for another official who had passed the government exams in the same year as he. But Uncle liked to say that the demons had examined him more rigorously than any government exam.

He was in his eighties and short and fat and built like a rock. He had a round face, with broad cheeks and a weak chin that made his thick lips seem to protrude even more. His belly stuck out above his pants top. It was usually covered by the loose tunic all the Tang men wore, but today he had worn a special blue silk coat.

"Don't you know it's impolite to stare, boy?" Uncle grunted.

"Why are you doing it then, sir?"

He rapped my forehead with his knuckle. "This boy has character, at least." Everyone laughed, relieved. I had been accepted. Uncle turned to Father. "You're a lucky man, Windrider."

"Windrider?" I asked Father. "That's not your name."

"It is now," Father said. "I'll explain later."

It was a good thing that my father was with me. The thousands of miles I had crossed were nothing compared to the last mile or so between the docks and the town of the Tang people, *Chinatown*. I kept twisting my head this way and that to look at the hills until Father stopped. 'What's the matter?" he asked.

"Which one is the Golden Mountain?"

Father did not even look at me, but turned around to look at poor Hand Clap. "Those two years in the Middle Kingdom haven't changed you one bit."

"Oh, now," Hand Clap mumbled. He scratched at his neck in embarrassment. "After all, the truth's what you make it."

Uncle Bright Star snorted. "It's a good thing you don't keep the books."

Father clapped his hand on my shoulder. "Boy, you have to realize that there was never a flea that Hand Clap didn't call a horse, and there was never a horse that he didn't call an elephant."

"And there has never been a country big enough to hold the elephant that Hand Clap has seen," Lefty laughed. He was bent almost double, hefting my straw chest with his good hand as it rested on his back.

"You mean there's no Golden Mountain?" I was

disappointed and felt a little betrayed.

"Not that we've ever seen." Uncle Bright Star added more kindly, "Though we've often wished it."

"Oh," I said in a very small voice.

Father took my hand kindly. "But there's a lot left to the demons' land that we haven't seen. Maybe we'll run across it yet."

"And like I've always said, that will be the day that everyone in the world decides to use copper and not gold for money," Uncle said.

"Then we'll look for a mountain of copper," Father laughed.

"And we'll let Hand Clap be our guide," added White Deer.

"And I'll guide you, cousins, straight and true," said Hand Clap, "for there's nothing I can't do. I can dig up a mountain, drink up a lake, outrun the wind. . . ." Hand Clap rambled on.

Father took the opportunity to whisper to me. "Stick close to me, Moon Shadow, and don't be afraid."

To get to the Tang people's town, you see, we had to pass through the *Barbary Coast,* a place filled with brothels and saloons and gambling joints. Walking up the street, I nearly lost heart. To me, the wooden houses seemed like shells of wood which terrible monsters had spun about themselves. It seemed as if the monsters would break out any moment through the wooden walls and grab me. One demon building in particular was very bad. It was only a saloon, I learned later, but it seemed terrible to me: It reeked of vomit and cheap liquor and stale sweat. For a long time I would associate this smell with the homes of the demons.

A young white demon pushed through its doors. He was in strange clothes of black and white that were obviously dress-up. I wondered if he were some kind of special demon. I watched as he stumbled into the railing before the saloon and quietly sat down.

His eyes crossed. *"What are you looking at, you little"* —it sounded like *"chai-na-maan?"*

I looked at Father for a translation, but he had grown angry. Uncle Bright Star stepped in between us and bowed. *"No sabe. No sabe. So sorry."*

And the others gathered around us and began pushing us up the steep hill toward the safety of the town of the Tang people.

Suddenly, I felt as if I had come home. I can see the town of the Tang people even now in the late afternoon sun—not as it is now, full of souvenir shops and neon signs, but as it was then. The houses and the stores had all the right colors and shapes, for they had been built not by demons but by the Tang people. It looked much like the streets in Canton, the city in the Middle Kingdom from which I had sailed. The roofs of the buildings here were tiled and arched, and the walls, windows, and doorways were in gold or red or green. Before the fronts of the buildings were sensible safeguards against demons of any kind. There were lions lying down protectively before some; other houses had pictures of the door guardians on their doors, and still others had scrolls of red paper on the doorways, asking a certain god to protect the inhabitants against demons.

On the blank walls of some buildings were long, narrow strips of red paper upon which words had been painted in thick, black ink. My father told me that some of them were advertisements, offering a heavy winter coat for sale, or somebody's services in writing a letter home, or perhaps a request to buy a demon watch. Above the posters and storefronts were balconies upon which men lounged, their faces turned toward the sun and their shadows arching behind them on the walls like long tails.

There was a breeze blowing down the hill and the men had gathered outside, standing on the sidewalks, their hands behind their backs, talking amiably. In their dark tunics and pants, they looked like shadows—a street of shadows, flitting here and there, talking in high, loud, excited voices. (People who think the Tang people are quiet have never listened to us in our own homes, where the conversation is carried on at the level of a shout.) And from some room far above the street came the lonely, peaceful sound of a moon guitar.

The streets were narrow, and the tall, three-story buildings on either side made them seem even narrower. Vendors shuffled along in the dusty streets because the sidewalks were too crowded. Over their shoulders the vendors had heavy poles, from which they balanced baskets at either end—some with vegetables, others with pastries, or candies, or toys. Their loads seemed heavy enough until the demon wagons rolled toward them, pulled by the huge-bodied demon horses with their breaths blowing and the sweat glistening on their flanks. Then the vendors had to dodge nimbly to avoid being trampled under the heavy hooves, while the demon drivers shouted largely unintelligible curses at them.

There were groceries and herbal shops, clothing shops and laundries, halls that housed the brotherhoods or the district associations or the offices of family clans. Uncle pointed out the building of the district from which my family came and to which I could go for help. Besides that, there was the Lee family building, which would help everyone who was named Lee.

But most interesting to me were the men who sold

their products from the stalls on the street. There was a butcher who worked in the mouth of a narrow alley. Behind the butcher were cages with fresh chickens waiting to be killed for the buyer, and before him was a big zinc washbasin filled with fresh fish. In one cage by his feet was a wildcat for some man who wanted to regain some of his youthful vigor.

There were men in long narrow stalls set against the sides of buildings who sold toys and different candies—one a type of sweet but hot-tasting, candied ginger that was a bright orange-red in color. There were dried fruits that you could buy—sweet, semi-sweet, or salty. These you sucked inside your mouth till all the flavor was gone, and then you stripped the moistened meat away from the seed. There were apricot candies pressed flat into wafers; thin, white, curled strips of coconut candy; several kinds of disclike rice cookies; and so on. And in the doorways men sat on the stoops selling various newspapers gathered in piles around them.

I should say now that there were no women on the streets, only men, thousands of men; and perhaps carefully locked away in the buildings might be a few hundred Tang women. Most of the women who came to the demon land were prostitutes. Oh, there were a few rich merchants who had brought their wives over with their maids, but these were the exceptions, and the wives had to be locked up even more carefully than the prostitutes to keep them from being kidnapped by some brotherhood and put to work in a brothel in another city.

We stopped before a small, neat, three-story building painted bright red and green. On the front of the building was a huge sign on which were painted Tang people's symbols and demon words, announcing to the whole wide world that this was the Company of the Peach Orchard Vow. The demons always thought the name was funny. Uncle let them laugh. It was Uncle who told me that the Peach Orchard Vow was a famous vow, taken by the man who became the god of war and his two sworn brothers, to serve the people and help one another. On the door were painted the names of the two door guardians who kept the demons away. And on the windows were painted the words for Long Life and Prosperity.

With a flourish, Uncle opened the front door for me and ushered me inside. "A superior home for superior men," he said. Uncle was fond of the phrase "the superior man," which he said he had taken from the wise man Confucius.

I stepped in and looked around. The air inside smelled of soap and food and sweat. The bottom floor was given over to the laundry. The washing was done in the basement and in the back half of the first floor. A long curtain shut the back half off from view. In the front half, the half where I was now, there was a circular stove, with a broad rack on top, that stood in the middle of the floor. Spare flatirons heated up on the rack. When a man's iron cooled, he took another from the rack and put the cold one back on the rack to reheat. On the walls to either side of the stove and within reaching distance were ironing boards that folded down from the wall itself.

On the walls above the ironing boards were strips of thick, bright red paper with poems and sayings on them. Since the words of the Tang people were more alive—more like pictures, really—handwriting was more of an art form than among demons. All the poems and the sayings were done in lively, or lovely, hands. The most delicately written poem had been done by Lefty when he still had his right hand. It was a poem written by the Drunken Genius, Lee the White, who drowned one night when he tried to embrace the moon as it appeared on the lake. The poem went like this:

> Upon my bed
> Lies the bright moonlight
> Like frost upon the earth.
>
> Lifting my eyes,
> I see the bright moon.
> Closing my eyes,
> I see home.

The poem hung above Lefty's ironing board.

There were other, more conventional pious sayings up on the walls. Ones like: "Peace and prosperity upon this store." They had been written by a man who had belonged to the Company before us. And there was one strip, faded and smoke-smudged by time, which had been written by one of the men who had founded the Company and who was long since dead. The founder had written: "The three virtues of the Stranger are to be silent, to be cunning, but above all to be invisible." Uncle told me that the warning had been taken from one of the Middle Kingdom's oldest books, "Classic of Changes."

All of us went up the stairs that led to the second floor. This was used as a kitchen and relaxation room, where the Company could read or gossip or play Mah-Jongg, the game with tiles that is something like the demons' card game of *gin rummy*. On the third floor were our sleeping quarters.

The dinner we had that night was the finest I had ever had. White Deer was the cook. He was a devout

Buddhist who ate no meat and so few vegetables that I doubt if a grasshopper could have lived on what he ate. Still, he was one of the finest cooks around.

At sixty, White Deer was the second oldest in the Company. Technically speaking, White Deer, Uncle, and Hand Clap were all partners. (Hand Clap had originally sold his share of the laundry to the other two when he had returned home to the Middle Kingdom, but now that he had come back to the Land of the Golden Mountain, he had bought back his share.) Lefty, Black Dog (Uncle's son), Father, and I only worked for wages till the day we could buy a junior partnership. But White Deer and Hand Clap never lorded it over any of us. We were all equally under Uncle's orders.

At any rate, White Deer outdid himself that day. He made duck with the skin parted and crisped and the meat salty and rich and good. He had cooked squab in soy sauce so that the skin and meat were a deep, deep brown all the way to the bone. There was shark's-fin soup, tasting of the sea. There were huge prawns fried in a special batter that gave them an extra fluffy coat. And on and on. But we weren't allowed to touch any of the courses until we had the toasts.

Lefty raised a cup of wine in his left hand. His right arm he held behind his back, as he often did. Hand Clap had warned me beforehand not to stare. Like many another lonely man, Lefty had taken up gambling the way others might have taken up drinking or dope: It was something to fill in the long, empty hours. As Hand Clap had told me, Lefty bought his ticket home, but the night before he was to leave, he tried to double his money. Not only did he lose all his money, but his ticket home as well. In despair the next morning because he would not see his family for at least another five years, he had taken a cleaver and cut off his right hand—the hand that had held the dice.

Lefty came from Canton, so he spoke a different dialect from ours. There was a kind of polish on Lefty, which is perhaps why he was picked to give the toast. Lefty held up his cup of wine. The wines of the Tang people are of a very high alcoholic content, and much stronger than demon wines. In fact, the sixty-proof demon *brandy* was what Uncle called wine. "A toast," Lefty said, "to our youngest brother, Moon Shadow, the son of the brilliant Windrider. May Moon Shadow work hard. May he become rich soon. May he return home even sooner."

Everyone drank to that. Uncle tossed his drink back in one gulp. "Dry cup," he announced, and turned his cup upside down. Not one drop was left inside to fall down. He smacked his lips. "My, my, but that is a righteous wine. I'll have another."

When Uncle's second cup had been poured, he looked at me. "Boy, this Company was here a year before I even came to the land of the demons, and it was operating successfully for twenty years before I finally joined it. It will go on after me, for this Company is an idea. It is a dream—a dream that is much older than you or I and only slightly younger than the world: Men must help one another in dangerous times and places."

"Yes, now to the Company," Hand Clap said. We all drank again. Again Uncle shouted, "Dry cup," and held his cup upside down.

White Deer dumped a big spoonful of rice into Uncle's bowl. "Here, old man, better get something on that stomach of yours before you get sick." If Uncle Bright Star was the father to us, White Deer was something like a mother. We all set to eating then. The talk around the table was about our villages and events in the Middle Kingdom, especially now that the Boxer Rebellion was over for good. But eventually, things came around to what Hand Clap had missed in the demons' land.

It turned out that the mad "socialist," *Theodore Roosevelt,* was going to run for reelection. He had been vice-president at the time when the real president, *McKinley,* had been shot in a provincial city. It was the only way, Uncle solemnly declared, that the crazy demon could have gotten into office. To Uncle's mind, *Roosevelt* was always trying to wreck the big companies. Uncle was against any tampering with business—even those belonging to demons.

Finally, when everyone had eaten his fill and could not touch another morsel, Uncle announced it was time for the presents. Lefty and White Deer went upstairs. When they came back down, they told me not to look behind me.

"Our young man must be properly attired." Lefty jammed a black hat down over my eyes. "That should keep the sun off that girlish skin of yours."

I pulled up the brim and took it off and looked at it, smoothing the crown. "Thanks, " I said, "but are you sure you won't be needing it to keep the sun off that nose of yours?"

The Company all laughed uproariously at that. Even Lefty goodnaturedly rubbed his nose. "Well, I might just take it back, boy, to hang it on my nose, so best keep an eye on it."

White Deer put a tunic and trousers on the table. "These are from me," White Deer said. "I hope they fit."

"If not, we'll cut him to fit the clothes," Father said.

"And these are from me to keep those calloused

farmer's feet of yours from wearing out the demons' streets." Uncle Bright Star clomped a pair of boots onto the table. "Actually, you're to wear these only when the rain comes, so don't waste the leather in the dry times." Uncle sat back, satisfied, as I admired the shiny black leather.

"Now let's see what the Windrider has for his son." Father spread his hands on the table. "I don't have anything nearly as fine as these things," he said. "Why, the Emperor himself would be proud to clothe his son in such fine raiment."

"Well, the Emperor's son will just have to go naked," Hand Clap shouted and they laughed and hooted at that, for there was no love lost for the present Emperor, who was a Manchu, a son of the foreigners who had conquered the Middle Kingdom and who long ago made us wear queues as a sign that we had been beaten by them. The queues were supposed to imitate the tails of horses, as if we were animals who had been tamed. It was death for any Tang man to wear his hair short. Of course, over a period of two hundred and sixty years a lot of Tang men no longer knew what the queue had originally symbolized. They could be quite vain about the care of their queues, but that did not mean they loved the Manchus.

"Go on, fetch your silly toy." Uncle jerked his head at the stairs. With a secret smile, Father disappeared up the stairs. I heard his boots mount the steps heavily. He came down the steps a moment later from his third-floor room. Under his arm he had a kite. But what a kite!

The frame of light bamboo sticks had been bent, tied, and glued into the shape of a butterfly, and then the frame had been covered with rice paper, which is a thin, translucent kind of paper. The paper had been painted in bright blue and green colors. It seemed to tremble in Father's hands. I could see the jets of the gaslights through the tissue-thin paper. The kite seemed to glow and vibrate as if it were alive and breathing in my father's hands. I knew it would fly well when I tried it.

"It's just a little something," Father said casually.

"Be careful with it," Uncle warned. But I did not need to be told that. I would sooner have broken my arm—maybe even sooner. Arms can heal, but not wings like these.

"What do you say, boy?" Uncle poked me in the ribs.

"Thank you, Father," I said. I wanted to tell him about all the marvelous times I had had flying his kites, but I did not know how.

Father rumpled my hair affectionately. "You're welcome, boy. They gave you things for your body. I gave you something for your soul."

At that moment the bell rang as someone came through the front door. We heard heavy boots come up the stairs. Everyone grew silent in the room. I knew it was Black Dog coming.

Black Dog was the son born of Uncle's second wife —Uncle had taken more than one wife, as was the custom. Black Dog was a strange, brooding man in his forties. Thanks to Uncle's hard work, Black Dog and his brothers and sisters had been raised in luxury back in the Middle Kingdom. He had resented it when his father had made him come to the Land of the Golden Mountain. All of a sudden, after living like a young lord, he found himself doing the most drudgelike work.

It had not helped matters that he had come during the time of the troubles, when the demons had roared through the Tang people's town claiming the

Tang people took jobs away from them. They beat up innocent Tang men, and hung others by their queues from the lampposts. Black Dog began to despise his own father. He began to hang out with the brotherhoods who ran the gambling and the prostitution and the drug trade in the Tang people's town, and who were constantly fighting each other over control of various shady activities. Finally, Black Dog had taken to opium. He worked during the day in an offhand, insolent manner, but there was a strangeness to his eyes whenever you spoke to him.

Now he stood in the doorway, his hands stuffed into his pockets beneath his huge jacket. He was as tall as Father, but paler, and there was a scar by his right temple that he had gotten in a sword fight.

"Where were you, boy?" Uncle demanded. "I told you we were all going to be down at the dock."

"It slipped my mind, Father."

He strolled into the room and picked at the pile of clothes and glanced at the kite. "They forgot one thing," Black Dog said. He reached under his tunic, which went all the way past his waist. He tossed a demon's steel knife onto the table.

Father swept it up quickly. "I'll hold this for you till you need it."

"He may need it soon," Black Dog said. "The demons are all getting drunk and getting ready for beating up Tang men. The word is out to stay inside."

Right then we all heard the sound of a glass window shattering. Uncle led the way down the steps. The left window had been broken and the glass lay scattered across the floor. I was closest to the right window when the brick came through it. I stared at the brick as it slid across the clean, worn, wooden floor, and at the glass that scattered about my feet. Outside I could hear jeers and shouts. For one moment I glimpsed howling, sweating, red-and-white faces, distorted into hideous masks of hatred and cruelty, a sea of demon heads that bobbed restlessly outside our store. I could not understand the words they were growling out, but their intention was plain. They wanted to burn and loot and hurt. Looking into that huge mass of faces was like looking into the ugliest depths of the human soul.

By the light of the gas lamps in the street, I could see the Company. They all wore the same proud, silent expression. They had all been through this before. The demons called out things in their tongue. Father's face flushed, and he clenched and un-clenched his fists.

Hand Clap sighed. "Maybe now they'll get tired of us."

"They usually do," Uncle observed. "They'll go after fresh game now." He shook his head. "But these are bad times when one wishes all one's troubles on one's neighbors."

There came the sound of more windows breaking farther on down the street. With more shouts, the demons began to drift away, until only a few remained in front of our store. But even these left soon enough.

White Deer turned to Father. "Look at Moon Shadow. He's dying to see your room."

"You'll need help boarding up the windows and clearing up this mess," Father said.

Uncle waved his hand. "No, no, Windrider. Show the boy your room."

"Welcome to the land of the demons, boy." Black Dog laughed grimly. The glass crunched underneath our feet as we walked toward the stairs.

Chapter 3

The Dragon Man
(April, 1903)

As Father led me up the stairs, I forgot about the demons, for I began to wonder again about his name, Windrider. Every Tang man can have several names. He has a family name and a personal name given to him at birth. He can have another name given to him when he comes of age, a nickname from his friends, and if he is a poet, he can have a pen name. We are not like the demons, who lock a child into one name from birth— with maybe a nickname if he is lucky. We feel that a man should be able to change his name as he changes, the way a hermit crab can throw away his shell when it's too small and find another one.

When Father stopped before our door, I asked him, "Why do they call you Windrider?"

"Wait," he said. "You'll see. It's really a name I had before I was born in this life."

He pushed open the door. He waited almost shyly by the doorway as I went inside. The room was only about ten feet wide. By one wall were two mats and a trunk. A large, long table filled the opposite wall, while shelves covered the other two walls. There were piles of the strange, thick, cloth-like paper of the demons on one corner of the table. (I was used to the much thinner rice paper of the Tang people.) Every other inch of space in the room was crowded with small, strangely constructed machines whose purpose I could not guess. I did not dare touch a thing. I thought that each machine was like a magical bottle or box, with demons waiting inside to burst out.

But then Father became as excited as a small boy. He showed me each item, handling the strange machines as if he had tamed whatever demons were trapped inside. (Though, even so, if I had been left alone in that room, I would have bolted.)

Father motioned to a demon machine whose guts lay scattered around a board. There were lumps of crystal connected by wires and other things. It looked like some strange, magical pattern of great power. There was a wire band with a circular disc at either end. On the board was painted the word for sharing. I found out why when I heard of the Dragon King's throne. Father pointed to the band and discs. "Those are *earphones*." He touched the board. "This is a *crystal set*. Through this we can talk through walls and across the city. They've already talked across the ocean."

"Across the ocean?"

"Yes."

"Can you talk to the Middle Kingdom?"

Father's face softened. "No, boy. It was the demons' other ocean."

Then Father showed me a device which he called an *electric light*. It consisted of a stand in which was set a globe of clear glass. Inside, filaments of burnt bamboo perched like a black insect. The guts of the light—they were really wires—led from the globe across the table, vanishing into the jumble of machines.

Father dimmed the gaslight. "Watch this," he said eagerly. He examined the table, gave a grunt when he found what he wanted, and turned a switch. I heard a click. Suddenly the insect within the globe shone with a light that was so bright and intense that it hurt my eyes, and I cried out.

Father turned off the switch. "What's wrong?"

I didn't say anything, but Father realized I was scared from the way I was shaking. He put his arm around me and I felt his reassuring bulk. He waved his free arm around at the room. "All of these things are only toys. They're harmless."

"Because you learned the demons' magic to protect you?"

Father smiled and laughed softly. "No. No. What's here belongs neither to us nor to the demons. It's only a form of a much greater and purer magic. It can do harm in the hands of a wrong man and lash back on him; but the superior man need not be afraid."

But he could see from my face that I was not too sure about the devices in the room. He sighed and scratched the back of his head as if puzzled. "Won't you take my word for it, boy?"

"It's hard to order someone to believe." I added, "Sir." We both felt stiff and awkward.

Father spread his hands. "Oh, hell, boy. I don't know much about being a father."

"I guess I don't know much about being your son," I said slowly.

"Yes, well," he nodded to me. "I guess we'll have to learn together then." He sat down on the mat. "But I can see I'll have to tell you about my name. Then you'll understand why you should not be afraid." He patted a place beside him. I sat down there. He nodded his head at the devices on the table. "All of those are part of my name. The story was told to me by the Dragon King himself."

Of course, not all dragons are evil, as I later discovered the demons think they are, for they can be good to you as well as bad. In fact, most dragons are good creatures who bring rain to the farmers when they soar up from the water and fly through the sky. Dragons can be kindly and wise, and quite unlike the firebreathing, malicious, greedy creatures the white demons seem to think dragons are. There are some dragons that delight in harming other creatures, even their own kin. But the Dragon King himself is by and large a good creature who rules over all reptiles and the animals who live in the sea, and some say he is the head of all the other animals. The Dragon King is one creature you stay friends with, since he can cause earthquakes as well as floods and droughts. To have him personally tell you a story is quite an honor.

"You never wrote to us about the Dragon King," I said.

"It's hard to put such things into a letter, especially when the letter is read to your family by another person."

I nodded, understanding.

Father settled back against the wall. He put his hands behind his head so that his arms were bent and looked like wings. His face took on a strange expression—one I was to see only a few more times in the years to come. It was as if he were in another world and describing it to me—as if he were actually there seeing and hearing and feeling what was going on.

"That first night," Father said, "that I had come to this land, there had been a feast for the group of us that had just arrived on the boat. Because of the late hours telling stories and the drinking, the others slept deeply, so no one could tell me the next day if I had really left."

Father's story went like this:

I had gone to sleep with the others, but I woke up to find myself on a strange beach. I scooped up some of the sand and saw that it was really tiny sapphires that made noises like laughter when I rubbed some of them between my palms. Behind me rose steep-sided mountains of amber, on which had been carved words of great power to try to bind the creatures who lived within. The giant animals moved about inside the mountains dimly, like shadows, huge, terrible shadows. The sea itself was still and calm. There was not the slightest surge of surf, and no wind stirred its surface. It was a strange, deep, troubling shade of green, as if it held the sunlight rather than reflected it.

Then I looked around the beach and saw, drawn up in ranks, regiment after regiment of strange, silent, scaled soldiers, but I paid little attention to them. For there, lying in the middle of the beach, was a great dragon, perhaps five hundred yards long.

His great head lay pillowed against a sand dune and a dozen or more soldiers waved their wicker shields, trying to fan cool air upon him. His head was long and shaped like that of a horse or a camel, with the great nostrils widened as he tried to breathe. His horns were like those of a deer, but they looked as if they had been carved of ivory. There were streamers of the red flesh of some luckless opponent still clinging to some of the points, though other soldiers were trying to clean them off. His ears were forked and twitched like those of a rabbit. His body was as long and powerful as that of a snake, but he had four heavy, squat legs. The pad of each foot, though, was leather hard. Because this dragon had five gold-tipped claws, I knew him for the Imperial Dragon, for only royal family have five claws. All the other dragons are born with only four. In the middle of his forehead was a great pearl, which gleamed like the moon on a cold, crisp autumn night; but its luster was fading. His vast chest heaved up and down and his wings were folded onto his sides. The fine golden whiskers of his beard were still flecked with blood and his own sweat. He was also growing bald for a dragon: He was so old that the scales at the top of his head had begun to flake off and expose the soft, golden skin beneath.

The Dragon King opened his great eyes, eyes perhaps ten feet in diameter. Old they were, and sad and wise, and yet gentle at the same time. But they looked like two deep wells of golden light—deep enough to swallow the whole world, it seemed. No one could look long into the eyes of the Dragon King. I knelt and pressed my face against the sand.

"Humph," he grunted, "rather a miserable, soft-skinned body they've given you, Windrider." The Dragon King's voice boomed inside his vast body, the words echoing and vibrating like a gong in a large hall. "You committed a great crime, but you at least deserved to be born as a worm or a lizard. I mean, really, it's a bit drastic to be born as a softskin, don't you think?"

"I don't know," I said, still not daring to look up.

The Dragon King sighed. "You made terrible puns, cheated at dice, and criticized the meter of my excellent poems, but you were once a phenomenal healer."

"But my Lord," I quavered, "I am only an ignorant man who knows nothing of the art of healing."

I felt a great shower of sapphire sand as his head rose up. The Dragon King laughed, and it sounded like someone pounding on a brass door. "Aha. Aha. Aha. My dear fellow, right now you may be as miserable a specimen of a softskin as it has ever been my misfortune to see; but in a former life, you were once the greatest physician of all the dragons, and—I must tell you—something of a show-off when it came to flying. That's how you got your name. Then, in one of your playful moods, you grew as large as the world and tried to blow out the fires in the sun by fanning your wings. For that great crime, your head was cut off and you were reborn among the softskins. And among them you must remain until you prove yourself worthy once again of being a dragon."

"But I remember nothing."

The Dragon King sighed patiently. "Before a soul is reborn into a new body in a new life, he drinks a broth which makes him forget everything. But though your mind might not remember, your hands do. My spies tell me you still retain some of your old skills."

"But I know nothing of healing, my Lord. I only tinker with machines."

"I am never wrong." I felt the Dragon King wag a claw above my head. "Surely you remember that the magic of our kingdom takes different forms in the mortal lands? Once, as a dragon, you could cut the small shapes of butterflies and birds out of paper and make them come to life. Now as a softskin you can only make the things called kites—that skill is only a remnant of your old powers." I heard him lower his head again onto the sand. He let out another sigh and the sand blew about me. "Now heal me, for I grow weary of our talk."

"I will try my best, Lord."

"Trust to your hands and do not think about what you are doing." The Dragon King added, "And do not fear. No harm will come to you if you fail. I called you here as my old friend."

All this time I had kept my face to the sand, but I took courage from his words. When I felt a great shadow pass over me, I looked up. The Dragon King had spread his left wing outward to reveal the wound in his side. The bony ribs of the wing stood out as high as a hill, and the arteries and veins gleamed like wires of finespun ruby and turquoise pressed into a thin sheet of jade. But then I looked at his side and saw a gash that was about twice as long as me. It had been covered with an ugly black scab. He told me later he had received the wound during a border skirmish with the outlaw dragons who lived in the hills of the seashore.

"I cannot work on you when you are this big, Lord. You must reduce yourself to . . . oh . . . about twelve feet."

The Lord dwindled in size until he was only about twice my length. Without thinking, it seemed, my hands knew what to do, as if there were some residue of my old memories still left in my hands, if not in my mind. The soldiers brought a medicine chest. I mixed a liquid and said the proper prayers and washed my hands. Suddenly my hands were as transparent as the finest glass. It was only by holding my hands at a certain angle in the sunlight that I could even see them. The flesh of the Lord suddenly became as nothing. By touch alone I fitted bones together and fused them. Then I knitted the bone back to the sinew and the sinew back to the tissue. Finally I pressed a poultice of certain herbs over the whole wound, using a trowel-like instrument to plaster it on.

When I washed my hands in the sea, my hands became solid again. Then I removed the poultice. The flesh of his chest was as smooth as the rest of his skin. There was not even a scar.

"Ah," sighed the Dragon King. In his exuberance, he swelled up to his former gigantic size. "How can I ever reward you?"

I knelt humbly before him.

"Make me a dragon again, Lord, as you say I once was."

"Windrider, I would do it with all my heart, but that I cannot do," said the Dragon King. "You must wait until you have lived out your allotted span as a mortal. And you may not become a dragon again—much as you or I would wish it—unless you prove yourself worthy to be a dragon once more, and you can only do that by passing a series of tests that will be given to you as a softskin. Behave as a true dragon and you will pass them all, and by so doing, you will be given your true form. But it will be no easy task, for you may not know you have been tested until after it is over."

The Lord tapped his claws on the ground. It was only a thoughtless little tapping for him, but the ground rumbled underneath the rest of us. "Ah. But I can show you about our dragon kingdom so you'll want to return. It will also be a fine excuse to keep you here for a little while. I don't think my family would forgive me if I sent you away before they had a chance to drink to your health." And he smiled a twenty-yard-long smile.

At the Lord's command, a squad of soldiers brought a set of shimmering wings, shaped like a dragonfly's, of some thin, transparent stuff stretched over a framework of gold wire.

"These are wings, if you have the courage to use them," the Lord said.

I looked dubiously at the wings. They seemed fragile things. But I was ashamed to let the Lord see me frightened after all the things he had said about the former me.

I took off my shirt as I was told and knelt in the sand. From a jar a soldier took a sweet-smelling paste and smeared it on my back along the shoulder blades. Immediately my back began to itch.

"Do not scratch," the Lord warned me

sternly.

Then a pair of soldiers brought the wings. I felt a prodding at my back as if someone were pushing two sticks against it. Then I felt a tugging sensation. I turned around to see the soldiers pulling at the wings on my back as if they wanted to make sure they were securely fastened. Then the soldiers backed away. I stared in amazement.

"Stand up, Windrider."

I did, or at least I tried to; but I nearly fell on my back because of the weight of the wings. They weren't heavy, mind you; but it was the change in my balance. I found later that by leaning forward I would be all right when I got up.

I tested the wings timidly at first. There was only that thin, bone-like rib around either wing to give it structure. The ribs felt as if they were as hollow as the quill of a feather. The wings themselves were finer than the finest rice paper, and yet they were strong. Once during my trip, a flock of birds came out of a cloud bank. I managed to dodge most of them, but some of them hit my wings. Poor things—they broke their necks against my wings. But that happened later.

Right then I spread my wings and saw the glory of them! They had been gold at first, but now I saw how they shone iridescently— like the rainbow colors you see on a soap bubble if you look at it from the right angle. The colored light shimmered and shone on the wings' surface and I flexed them joyfully, delighted with how the colors spread and played upon their surfaces.

"Now," the Lord said proudly, "use them."

I tried waving them lightly and felt myself spring into the air, to hover above the Lord's head.

"Easy," the Lord cautioned me. "You don't want to tire yourself out."

I did a loop. I did a long, slow glide. It was a heady feeling. The world spun out below. I flew so high that the beach looked just like a strip of blue paper set down beside a pane of green glass that was the sea. I looked up and there was nothing between myself and the gods in heaven but sky—lovely, blue sky. I flew around in great, lazy circles, delighted with my freedom.

"Is it good to be back in the sky, Windrider?" he shouted up to me.

"Yes," I shouted back.

And then the Lord rose from the beach. There is no more awesome sight than a dragon first taking flight. He tilted up his head and tensed his legs. Then with one great beat of his wings, he sprang into the air.

You have to picture what it was like to see that great mountain of flesh suddenly uncurl and rise into the sky. A giant column of muscle and flesh suddenly leaped upward— ton after ton of flesh suddenly pouring itself skyward in defiance of gravity. He shot by me and I got caught in his tail stream as he went past. I tumbled head over heels, but I soon righted myself in time to see the greatest aerial display a man will ever see. Though I do not think he would have admitted it, I do believe he wanted to show off too.

The Lord flew effortlessly, twisting his

body in curls and spirals the way a skilled dancer can take a twenty-foot ribbon and make it form graceful designs behind her. The Lord seemed to be signing his name in the sky with all the right lines and swelling strokes.

And then he came up beside me. "Now, Windrider, we will fly through my kingdom to your real home."

He was old, that dragon, but his heart was young. On the way to his kingdom, we had races—short ones, out of consideration for me. After all, I only had puny softskin muscles now to power my wings, while he had the muscles of a dragon's body. Sometimes we raced so low that our feet broke the surface of the water and we plowed great white wakes behind us, and we would end the race by tracing designs in the sea.

It would take me all night to describe the dragons' kingdom and all the great creatures that live there. And what can I say of the jeweled dragon palaces or of the undersea gardens? They had fountains, not of water but of air, among other wonders. I could go on for days and days about everything I saw in his palace, but the meanest rooms there, which were assigned to the scrubdragons, were worthy of human emperors.

But the thing I remember most was the Dragon King's throne. It must have stretched for several acres, and to support all of his bulk there were a hundred golden legs, each carved like some creature of the sea. The throne itself was of pure, unalloyed gold, and since pure, unalloyed gold is almost as malleable as clay, a crew of dragon goldsmiths was kept busy all the time repairing the throne where the Lord might have dented it. He settled himself on his throne, laying himself down in coil after careful coil. The arms and back of his throne were encrusted with all kinds of gems, each as big as my fist.

Among all those precious jewels on the back of his chair there was a plain black stone above his head. The Lord showed it to me. On it was the word for sharing, and when it was set into a certain design—with one long nail, the Lord delicately traced the design on his throne—it would let you speak to whomever you named. It helped the Lord to keep track of his vast realm.

He spoke into the stone, calling all of his nine sons and daughters and his twenty-seven grandchildren and his eighty-one greatgrandchildren to meet Windrider again that night at a feast. When he was finished, he let out a sigh. "I tell you, Windrider, with each year, it gets harder to remember all the names."

"Yes," I said absently. I looked up wistfully at the chair.

The Lord finally understood. "Whom would you like to hear, Windrider?" he asked gently.

"My wife," I said.

I spoke her name into it, and all of a sudden I heard your mother singing a lullaby to you as you gradually stopped crying. You must have just been born, for I as yet had had no news of your birth.

"You could speak to them," the Lord said.

"No," I said. I'm afraid that I began to cry.

"I don't want her to feel what I feel, listening to her but not being able to touch her. Better that she shouldn't know."

"As you wish," the Lord said, and quickly distracted me by challenging me to a game of dominoes. I won—he grudgingly admitted that I had won by skill and not by cheating. He told me he would hold my winnings for when I was reborn again as a dragon.

But finally it was time for me to return to my mortal world. It was reluctantly that the Lord said good-bye to me and added, "We will save a place at the banquet table for you. You will be eating with us soon, though, if you just remember to watch for the tests and hold to the dragon-ness within that softskin body. Now fare you well."

Father sat in silence for some time.

"The others say it was a dream. The only proof I had was my sore back and ribs the next day. And that is no proof. Uncle said I must have gotten up and fallen sometime in my sleep."

"I believe you were there, Father." I touched his arm shyly. "Something as beautiful as that has to be true."

Father smiled in our newfound understanding. "Then we must both be as true as dragons can be and must not try to put out the sun."

Looking at his smile, I felt as if here at last in the city of the demons, I had found my true father, and more—a friend and a guide.

Later that evening, as I lay on my mat, I heard a sound like a great bear shuffling down the hall. There was a tap at the door. I opened it to see Uncle.

He looked down at me.

"Thought you'd be up," he pretended to grumble. "This is just a little knickknack I made in my spare time. If you don't want it, just throw it away." He tossed something over onto my mat and left. I went over to my blankets and held the object up in my hands toward the dim light coming in from the gas lamp in the hall. It was a wooden carving of Monkey, the creature born of a stone egg who became king of all the monkeys and who almost conquered Heaven with them. No one else knew who had carved it. I never explained to anyone how I got it, not even to Father when he asked. I thought Uncle would want it that way. I figured out later that he must have carved it late at night when the others had gone to sleep. I can't say exactly why, except maybe Uncle was afraid of being laughed at by the others.

The object that he had treated so casually was beautifully meticulous. It was a work of art. In a better time and place, Uncle might have been a sculptor. It was only later that I saw how rheumatic Uncle's hands were, when he could sometimes barely grip his chopsticks. I realized then just how much effort it must have taken for him to hold a knife and wield it so painstakingly. It was more than a work of art. It was a work of love.

With that statue beside me, I fell asleep.

Chapter 4

Tests
(April, 1903–
February, 1904)

During the next year, I learned that the Company was more than a group of men wanting money. We were brothers: strangers in a strange land who had banded together for mutual help and protection. There were arguments, of course, but they were always worked out.

As for myself, I was treated as a man and not a boy; and the long hours I worked were really no worse than the hours I had worked on our farm. In the mornings I was the first to get up and make the fire and brew the tea for the others, and through the day there would be various things I would have to do. I did not go to school during the daytime like demon children because the demons would not allow me to go to any of their schools just a few blocks away. I could only go to a special school the demons had set up in the Tang people's town, which was so poorly equipped and so poorly staffed that I was better off in the Company.

All during the day, Uncle and Father would keep up a conversation with me using what they knew of the demons' tongue, and they made me read and discuss the demons' magazines and newspapers which some of our friends and kinsmen, who worked in the demons' mansions, would bring down to us. Demonic was easier to speak than to read. It was hard to understand a language that only used twenty-six symbols, the *letters* of their *alphabet*. The *letters* kept on rearranging themselves in the most confusing patterns.

At about four o'clock, after I had gotten the fire ready again for White Deer to cook dinner, I would hurry to the Tang people's school, where I would learn the classics of the Tang people. The classics were the books supposedly written by Confucius and the ancients, about the correct way to live. Some of them made sense. Some of them didn't. As Uncle told me, some of it applied to everyone, including demons, and other parts of it applied only to the rich.

When I came home two hours later from school, I would be in time to grab a quick dinner from the leftovers, wash the dishes, do my other chores and my lessons, and then go to bed. I worked sixteen hours a day and had never been happier in my life.

The part I liked best was when I went with Father to pick up the dirty laundry and deliver the clean. Because Father could speak more demonic than the others, he always got that job, and he usually took me along. Our wagon was painted a bright red, with the Company's name in demon script painted in large, bold gold *letters* on its sides. The wagon was pulled by Red Rabbit, whom we kept along with the wagon in a livery stable a few blocks away in the demons' section. Red Rabbit was a big, strong horse, red as fire, with a white star on his forehead. Father had named him Red Rabbit after the speedy horse of the god of war. As he jokingly said sometimes, he thought Red Rabbit would try to live up to his name; but so far the shameless beast had not. Red Rabbit was without a doubt the laziest, slowest horse in the demon land.

Uncle said half seriously that it was associating with demons that had made Red Rabbit so lazy. Whatever the reason, neither curses nor the whip nor kicks nor slaps of the reins on Red Rabbit's big rump could get him to move faster than his slow, deliberate pace—a pace which he never changed, whether we were in the flatlands or on one of the demons' steep hills. But no matter how slow he was, there was always a cube of sugar in my pants pocket.

In the beginning, Uncle had not wanted me to go out with Father and Red Rabbit. It was dangerous to leave the Tang people's town. There was many a Tang man with a cracked skull or a broken arm or rib because he had crossed over the invisible boundary line between our town and the rest of the demon city. Sometimes the demon boys threw stones, and other times it was a group of restless adult demons who were out for a little "sport."

But Father said it was time I learned a little more of the demons' city. I had already been here a month and never left the Tang people's town. He took me out only along streets that he regarded as safe, either because he knew the policemen on the beat or because some of his customers on that street had banded together and warned the demon boys and young men not to try anything.

The first time we went out, I had been afraid of just about everything. I remembered stories about how the hills were made by burrowing dragons, so I was scared to death by the sound the cable made going through the rails of the *cable car* tracks: a steady rattling, clacking sound. I thought it was a dragon scrabbling at the surface with its claws, just about to break free. As for the houses, they looked like wooden monsters, hunkered down along on either side, waiting for me to look away from them before they would grab me. And every demon I saw I was sure had a stone or a knife or a gun.

Father saw how I clutched the seat in sheer fright until the knuckles of my hands were almost bone white. Father began to speak quietly then of the Old Ones, the spirits of the dead members of our family to whom we offered food and the sweet smell of incense that pleased them so well. For their part, the Old Ones watched over the living members of the family, for one's obligations to the family did not stop with death.

Then Father spoke especially of the brave Old Ones who may have crossed over the sea to watch over us. Among these was my great-grandfather, who had died fighting the *British* demons when they had wanted to force the Tang people to let them sell opium in the Middle Kingdom. He was on the losing side and was beheaded for his trouble, but Father was sure that he for one would not miss a chance to fight demons again.

Father was even more positive that the spirit of my Grandfather was with us. I finally found out the truth about his death. He was a proud man who would take nonsense from nobody. One day shortly after he had arrived, some drunken demons had tried to cut off his queue. Grandfather could have worn a wig if his queue had been cut off. He would not have been the first "guest" of the demons who had to resort to one, but instead Grandfather had spat in their faces and busted a few heads, and before the whole thing was finished, he was swinging from a lamppost by some demon's clothesline.

Like many Tang men, he did not think of the queue as a symbol of Manchu oppression. Tang men had been wearing their hair in that way for over eight generations, so for Grandfather, having a queue was part of being a Tang man. He would as soon lose his nose as his queue. But even if he had been a revolutionary who knew what the queue really meant and hated the thought of wearing it, there was still the principle of the matter. The demons had no right to do anything to him physically. Anyway, I understood why Grandfather had died.

I let go of the seat, ashamed to let the Old Ones see how frightened I was. Father did not give me a chance to think about how afraid I should be. He would point with excitement at some new sight, or wonder with me at the meaning of something which we had seen among the demons. There were few things that escaped Father's notice, and even fewer things that Father was not interested in. Some of the houses had hitching posts cast in the shape of black demons, but in such odd clothes and of such odd colors that we never could figure them out. I learned later they were *jockey* clothes. Father and I speculated on the purpose of the figures—whether they were like the lions or the door gods who were meant to protect the house, or what.

When we started to make deliveries I was afraid of going near the houses, but I was even more afraid of being left alone on the wagon. I went with Father, feeling a certain pride in the Company's craft as I carried the clean, pressed, and starched clothes wrapped in the crisp, blue paper and tied with twine into neat parcels. And then I would help Father carry the dirty laundry back. If the bundle was small, say only about ten pounds, Father would let me carry it back to the wagon; but sometimes—especially when we were at some mansion—I had to let Father take the load.

While we did that, Father began to tell me about his life as a boy on our farm, his first years with Mother, and his first years over here in the demon land. But I liked it best when he sang, in his deep bass voice, some of the silly nonsense songs he and Mother used to make up when they were children. One of them he taught me went:

> The fox went a-walking,
> For to have a little flirt;
> But it made me so sad,
> For she had no skirt.
>
> The fox went a-walking
> Down by the sloughs;
> But it made me so sad,
> For she had no shoes.
>
> The fox went a-walking
> Down by the mall;
> But it made me so sad,
> She'd no clothes at all.

And it went on like that for dozens of verses, going through not only articles of Tang people's clothing but those of the demons as well—some of which, when we picked them up, amused us no end, especially the tons of petticoats and the like that demonesses had to wear. Father sang the song in such a mournful voice that he always made me laugh.

During those trips alone among the demons,

Father and I learned things about one another; and more, we learned about being a father and a son. Every trip was an adventure into a strange, fearful city; and yet I felt safe by my father's side. Anyone who could laugh and tell stories and jokes and sing while he was alone among the demons must know what he was doing. In my own mind, Father was the embodiment of Uncle's superior man.

Only once during all those trips did we have any trouble. Some demon boys were out in the street. They stooped as if to pick up things to throw, and Father whispered to me to sit up straight and not show I was afraid. The demon boys called out some things, but we ignored them until we had passed them by. A rock whizzed by my ear and hit Red Rabbit in the side. He snorted, but plodded on as steadily as before.

Then came that one fateful encounter with a demon. Because a demon can help or harm you, there is no way of telling if a demon might be testing you before he will reward you or whether he is trying to trick you. I had been in the demon land for only ten months, so it would have been about *January* of the demons' year 1904, when we met *Mr. Alger.* I remember it was a gray, wintry day. We were making the rounds when we saw one of the horseless carriages stranded by the sidewalk and a demon in a big overcoat standing beside it. His driving cap was pushed back, and he was scratching his forehead in a puzzled way. The metal hood on the front of the horseless had been folded back on top so you could see into its innards.

"Whoa, Red Rabbit." Father pulled at the reins and Red Rabbit stopped. Father set the brake, and as an extra precaution he put the wooden block behind the wheel.

"Can I help?" he asked.

The demon was a big, cheerful-looking demon with a bland, round face. He eyed father. *"I dunno, John."* Many demons called Tang men John because, they insisted, they never could get the hang of our real names. *"You know anything about horselesses?"* *"Some,"* Father said. Truth to tell, he had never handled a horseless carriage in his life, though he had a book on them and cut out articles whenever they appeared in the demon magazines and newspapers. That was the extent of Father's knowledge. But to know facts is nothing. He had an intuitive feeling for what made the horseless carriages tick. He looked around inside the engine for about ten minutes and then wiped his face absentmindedly, so that the grease stained his cheek. He did not even notice.

"Know where there's a garage?" the demon finally asked.

Father only grunted. His eyes were shining. He had hardly heard the demon until the demon tapped him on the shoulder. *"You sabe me? Garage. Repair my Oldsmobile."* As happens sometimes between two people speaking different languages, the demon had begun to shout at Father as if Father were deaf and the demon could make his words better understood by being loud.

But suddenly Father stiffened, hooked up a loose wire, and stood back. *"Horseless ready,"* he said with a satisfied air.

"What?"

"It ready."

Skeptically, the demon got back behind the wheel while Father went to the front near the crank to start the motor. Father put his thumb against his palm instead of putting it around the crank. As he told me later, when the motor took, the crank could move suddenly and break a man's thumb if his thumb was around it. He folded his hand carefully around the crank and began vigorously winding it. The motor caught and started with a chug. The whole horseless began to shake. Father closed the hood.

"*Here, John.*" The demon unbuttoned his coat and reached into his pants pocket, but Father shook his head.

"*No tip. Happy just to look at horseless.*"

The demon stopped and studied Father as you might look at a dog that had suddenly said he was going to the opera. "*Well, I'll be damned,*" he said. He reached into a pocket of his waistcoat and took out a card, and handed it to Father with a flourish. "*I can use honest handymen like you. You come around anytime, you sabe me?*"

"*Me sabe.*" Father nodded.

Father went to hold Red Rabbit's head as the demon wrestled the brake of his carriage free with a loud ratchety sound. Then he put the clutch in. There was the loud bang of a backfire and the horseless chugged forward. The demon grinned and waved. Father waved back. When Father climbed up beside me, he held out the card. "Here's a lesson for you," he said.

I puzzled out the words: "*O-li-ver Al-ger, Re-al Es-tate A-gent. Prop-er-ties sold and man-aged. One thousand two hundred Polk Street.*"

"Very good." Father took the card and put it carefully away in his pocket. "Did you see that demon's face, Moon Shadow? He was surprised when I fixed his carriage. Machines aren't all bad. Some of them may be the true magic. We might not be able to speak too well with the demons, but in machines there's a language common to us all. You don't have to worry about your accent when you're talking about numbers and diagrams."

I was getting excited. "Maybe the Dragon King was right. Maybe the magic takes a different form in our land. Maybe that's why you don't need words for it."

Father wiped his hands on an old rag in the back of the wagon. Then he held up his hands. He had not been able to get off all the oil, for the lines of his hands were still black. "Well, you know, repairing the horseless carriage was a lot like healing the Dragon King. My hands just seemed to know what to do."

I leaned forward eagerly. "Do you think that was the Dragon King in disguise? Do you think it was a test?"

Father gave my queue a friendly tweak. "You're too ready to find tests everywhere," he grinned. "Why can't he just be a demon?"

"But White Deer says there are good demons and bad demons. But was he showing us something good or bad? Was it—"

"You talk too much." Father clicked his tongue and shook the reins, and Red Rabbit started forward again.

But whatever Father said to me, his meeting with the demon made him look doubly hard through the demons' papers for signs of the true magic. It might have been that Father secretly took the meeting and the successful repairing of the horseless carriage as a test, but did not want to tell me. Or probably it was simply the change in the demon's attitude from being surly to being friendly that encouraged Father. At any rate, he studied the papers even harder than I did.

But not only did I have to learn the demons' language, I also had to learn how to measure time by two calendars. There was the demons' calendar, which was based on the movements of the sun with its fixed number of days and months and its seven-day weeks. And there was the true time of our own home, with its calendar based on the movements of the moon so that the first day of our New Year changed with each year, as did many of our holidays. Then, too, our week was ten days long.

But above all I wanted to learn Tang words so I could write Mother myself and be able to read her letters on my own; and there were a lot of letters, for she had begun to dictate twice a week to the schoolteacher. In her part of the letter, Grandmother had grumbled a bit about the expense—not that she begrudged us the extra letters, but their budget was a bit tight. But Mother in her part of the letter had argued that they now had twice as many loved ones to write to in the Land of the Golden Mountain. Father had told them that we would tighten our belts a bit over here and try to send on some extra money to cover the mail expenses. In the meantime, we had done our best to match them letter for letter so that they got their money's worth in return. Of course, in her next letter Grandmother had wanted to know how come we could suddenly afford to pay for double the mail load.

Grandmother became quiet, though, when I added my own lines to one of Father's letters. I first wrote to them in late *November* of the demon year 1903; but because of the distances, it took two months (a month for our letter to reach them and a month for their letter to reach us) for their reply to reach us. That would have made it the first month of our year 4061, but early *February* of the demons' year 1904.

Mother told us how proud she and Grandmother were. The schoolteacher himself had exclaimed over my handwriting and vocabulary—both of which I owed more to Lefty's private tutoring than to my teacher in school. My mother added that she wished I were there to help her go through our box of Father's old letters, for there were now many passages she had forgotten over the years.

I suddenly felt very guilty, for in all the excitement of slowly learning about Father and living in the demon land, I had not really had time to think about Mother. But now I remembered about how it used to be, sitting on the edge of the rice field as she waded through the brown, clouded water. I remembered, too, how after the dinner dishes had been washed and dried, we would sit by the small hearth and look at the fire and think of things that we ought to tell Father in our next letter, or how when we had come back from the schoolmaster, we would spread out one of Father's letters and pretend to read it to one another. Mother had always been good at that, for she would have the schoolteacher repeat a section she was not sure of—despite the schoolteacher's grumbling. When she got home, she could almost recite the letter by heart. She must have done the same thing with the parts of the letter that I had written.

"What's the matter, boy?" Father asked.

But as much as I would have liked to, I found it impossible to tell him about my feelings, though I think he suspected. He pretended to become very severe with me. "Now don't you go getting a swelled head by what the schoolteacher says, boy." And Father set me to reading the letter out loud, helping me with the more difficult words.

Then, after setting me to another lesson, Father went through a pile of old demon newspapers and magazines that one of our friends had brought down from some demon house in which he was employed as a houseboy. Suddenly Father waved the *"New York Herald"* magazine at me. It was a fairly recent one, dated January 17, 1904. I know the date because I still have it. One rich demon subscribed to the paper and had it shipped to him all the way across the country. It always boggled my mind to think of the great mountains and wide rivers across which he had people bring the papers just for his reading pleasure.

Father spread the magazine out before me. I saw a series of drawings of a boxlike contraption. Father pointed to the big letters beneath the picture. "This means the demon flew."

"Flew?" I said excitedly.

"That's what it says. A pair of demon brothers by the name of *Wright* flew in an *ae-ro-plane.*" Father's tongue rolled over the syllables. He pronounced the demon word again as if delighted with the sheer sound of the full vowels. "An *aeroplane.*"

"Were they given the wings by the Dragon King?" I asked.

Father laughed. "No." He tousled my hair affectionately. "Not so they say. They repair bicycles. But what some demon did, I can do." His eyes had gone as deep as they had when he had spoken of learning to fly on that strange beach.

The others were down on the second floor where our dining room-kitchen doubled as a gaming room in the evenings, when the dishes had been cleared away. Only Uncle was not excited by the demon magazine. He folded his arms across his chest and pondered his next move at the Tang people's chess, which is slightly different from demon chess (for one thing, there is a river across the board). Finally, Uncle pushed a chariot forward and sat back for White

Deer to make his move. "It's probably just some fairy tale for children," Uncle said. "You just haven't read it the right way."

"No, no, it's fact," Father insisted.

"You can't trust everything you read in the demons' papers," Uncle observed loftily. He was sitting in his special treasure, a chair which the founder of the Company had built and carved from teakwood brought all the way from the Middle Kingdom. The head of the Company always sat in that chair. Uncle treated his chair very much like a throne in which no one else was allowed to sit. When Uncle was settled into his chair, he did not so much speak as make proclamations, so we knew better than to argue with him at that time.

I could not understand why Uncle took such a stubborn attitude against the fact that some demon had flown. Father went to the demons' library and read through all the newspapers gathered from around the country, and he copied out the accounts of them. All of these Uncle refused to believe were true. But a few days later, we received our next sign. Melon Head was a laundryman in *Oakland*—he had gotten that name because he had gone completely bald in his younger days. He belonged to the same guild as we did and often caught the ferry over to attend the guild meetings. He was an old friend of Uncle's and usually dropped by our place afterward for a snack after he and Uncle had gone to the meeting.

Uncle was not feeling at his best that night. He had quarreled again with Black Dog—over what, no one knew, but Black Dog had walked out in a huff. Uncle's mood was not helped any by Melon Head's news.

Over tea he told us about some crazy demon,

Baldwin, who put air into a big canvas bag and then floated up into the sky, where he was under the control of the winds. He had a special, sausage-shaped canvas bag built for him, maybe about thirty feet long. It was covered with a giant net which went down to its belly, from which a wooden frame was suspended. There were *propellers* and a motor in the frame, and they sent the bag lumbering through the air, so he could guide his own flight.

It was one of the pioneer *dirigibles,* but at that time we thought of it as almost a miracle. It was called the *California Arrow,* though Red Rabbit was a rocket compared to it. The real crazy thing was that the demon was testing it so that he could race it at a big fair held at one of the demons' inland cities and maybe win some money in a contest being held for flying machines. The demon then planned to take it all around the demons' land and charge people admission to see him fly.

"Can you imagine flying and making money at it too?" I said wonderingly.

"No, I can't, because it's too risky to fly. Better to stay on the ground and do something you know you can make money at." Uncle spoke in his sternest voice.

"But supposing he does," Father said.

"You're crazy. First you wanted to bring your wife and your boy over to this place to live, and now you want to fly like a bird. Next thing I know you'll be collecting twigs for a nest."

"And you have a mouth that runs on, old man," White Deer snapped. It was one of the few times I had ever seen him look angry. "You weren't supposed to talk about that."

Uncle glanced first at me and then at Father guiltily. "I didn't—I mean—"

"You were going to bring Mother over as well?" I asked.

"The demons will let a merchant bring his wife over, but I have to be a partner in the store," Father said.

"But then how did you bring me over?" I asked.

"You came here as a merchant's son," Father said. "We got a paper saying that I was a partner in the store and owned a thousand *dollars* worth of property here; but that was only for the demons. I actually don't have a share in the store."

"But you could bring Mother over with that piece of paper."

Uncle cleared his throat. He did not like what he had to say. "Not while I'm the head of this Company. I'd go to the demons and tell them that the paper was a lie."

"But if the demons knew that Father wasn't a real partner in the store, they might send me home as well," I said. "And maybe the demons would even send Father back home because he lied."

"Yes, well." Uncle scratched uncomfortably at his ear and peered at the wall. "I'd rather lose both of you than see you bring your poor mother over here. What kind of place is this for her when we're afraid to set foot outside our own door?"

"You used to tell me how no one would ever fly either," White Deer pointed out, "and yet the demons are."

"And I bet the families of those demons are going hungry right now," Uncle declared smugly. "And all because of someone's crazy dream."

Father was going to argue with Uncle some more, but White Deer shook his head. There was no use going on. "Come," Father said to me. "It's time for you to go to bed." We said good night to Melon

Head and left.

I kept quiet when we got to our room, but it was obvious from my face that I wanted to talk. Father sighed. "Well, out with it before you bust."

"Were you really going to bring Mother over here?"

"It's only a dream of ours, Shadow," Father said gently. "Before I left home, your mother and I secretly agreed to do it if it could be managed; but I'm more likely to fly again in this life than to bring your mother over here."

"But perhaps you will fly," I said. "What better test of your dragon-ness than if you could fly in a softskin body? And if you could do that hard task, Uncle would have to believe you were once a real dragon, and then he would respect you even more than he does and he would do what you say. Then you could bring Mother over."

"You talk too much, boy." Father laughed, but he looked thoughtful. He pulled the quilt up about my neck. Then he turned the gas down on our gaslight. As I fell asleep, I could see him sitting on his mat, weighing the possibilities of what I had said.

The next day after we had had our morning rice, Uncle came over to Father. "Oh, my head." Uncle touched his fingers to his temples. "I drank too much wine last night."

Father grunted. He wet one finger and lifted an iron from the rack on the stove, where it had been heating. He tested it by putting his finger next to the iron. The moisture on Father's finger evaporated, making a soft sizzling sound, so Father knew it was ready without any discomfort to himself. He looked up from the iron. "You stiff-necked old goat," Father said. "Why don't you apologize and be done with it?"

Now Uncle was a proud man, and it had probably taken him most of last evening and this morning just to work himself up to this point where he would make excuses for his actions. But you could never force him to admit he was wrong. Uncle pressed his lips tightly together and his eyebrows drew closer together. "What makes you think I was going to say I was sorry?"

Father spread a shirt out on the ironing board. "I don't think when I'm around you. You do all the thinking for me."

"Well, someone has to. You can't be left on your own. A grown man your age playing with demon toys. You're a fool—a stupid, stupid fool—especially for wanting to bring your wife and family over to this place."

White Deer bent over and whispered in my ear. I could smell the soap on his hands. "Don't think too badly of Uncle. He's angry at his son and he grieves for him, but he holds all that anger and grief inside him. He's just taking those feelings out on the nearest person."

"But that still doesn't make it right."

"No, but neither would resenting Uncle's words. He doesn't mean them. He thinks your father's taken to flying the way that Lefty once was taken by gambling and the way that Black Dog is owned by his opium pipe."

In the meantime, the argument between Father and Uncle had reached the shouting point. "Go away, old man. Go away before I hit you with this iron," Father said. He turned away from Uncle and bent over the enamel bowl on the left side of the ironing board. He sucked his mouth full of water and then spat the water out forcefully in one large explosion, so that the entire shirt was sprayed with water. It was some way Father held his teeth and lips that made the water spray like that. Father very calmly began to iron.

Uncle snorted and stalked away.

But after ten days, Black Dog still had not come back. It was White Deer who joined Father beside his ironing board. "Black Dog's been gone a long time," White Deer said.

Father's arm went back and forth rhythmically across the sheet, smoothing out the wrinkles. "Yes, he has," he grudged.

"He's never been away this long," White Deer added.

"Unh," Father grunted.

"Opium costs too much. He's never had enough money for a binge as long as this."

"Unh."

"We ought to look for him."

Father sighed and set the iron he had been using back onto the stove rack. He took off another one that had been heating there and wet his thumb to test it. "I suppose we ought to," he said finally.

That night after dinner, Lefty began our confrontation with Uncle. "I understand that Leopard Head is down from the north country with his pockets full of money. I think I may get into a game." Leopard Head was a cook for the demons on some ranch up to the north The point was that he was a member of the Brotherhood of Eternal Repose, nicknamed the Sleepers (it was their enemies and not the brothers who rested eternally), the same brotherhood to which Black Dog belonged, and would be staying at their hall. If Black Dog was at the hall, Lefty could find out.

"If you see my worthless boy," Uncle grumbled, "spit in his face for me."

"No one is worthless, Uncle," White Deer chided him gently.

"He comes the closest to it of any Tang man I have ever seen." Uncle mopped his brow with his handkerchief. The air was still hot and steamy inside our building.

"He's probably too ashamed to come back," Hand Clap contributed.

"Yes, that's it," White Deer said. "He'll probably come back like a small dog with its tail slung between its legs."

"That boy knows no shame."

"He's still a member of the Company."

"Hah. I've got a good mind to fire that boy."

White Deer shrugged. "You can't fire someone from the Company unless your two partners agree, and Hand Clap and I will never do that."

But Uncle was still too proud to say he wanted help to look for his boy. "None of you are to look for him, understand?"

White Deer looked at his friend for a long time. "Well, there's no objection if I take a walk, is there?"

Uncle sat for a long time in his chair, drumming his fingers on the chair's arms. "No, I guess I can't keep you from going for walks." He pushed himself up from his chair suddenly. He picked his hat from a peg. "I think I'll visit Whirlwind. Haven't seen that old fool in a long time." Whirlwind also was a Sleeper. Uncle walked down the steps. The bell tinkled as he slammed the door.

"We ought to split up the rest of the Tang people's town," Father said. "I'll take the opium dens."

"No, let me," White Deer said.

"No," Father said. "It makes more sense for you to go among your friends in the restaurants and ask after Black Dog. He's got to eat sometime. Hand

Clap, you can cover the brothels. You know them all so well."

Hand Clap looked embarrassed when we all laughed. "Not that well," he mumbled.

"Leave the gambling places to me." Lefty slipped a silver dollar out of his pocket.

Father caught his wrist. "This is serious business, Lefty."

Lefty smiled. "Relax. I will not use this for gambling, only for buying drinks. There is nothing like wine to loosen tongues."

"All right." Father let go of his wrist.

"What about me?" I asked.

"Boy, you stay here."

"I want to go with you."

Father shook his head. "Where I'm going, nobody should have to go. What would your mother say?"

"Before I left, she told me to look after you. You'll need someone to watch your back for you."

"The boy is quite right, you know," Lefty said. "Some dopey may be just desperate enough to tackle you."

Father drummed his fingers on the countertop. "It's very ugly, boy. You'll think you're in the court of Hell."

"All the more reason to have someone you can trust there."

Father cocked his head to one side. "I do think you've grown an inch since you've come here."

"More like a foot," I said.

"You've been using Hand Clap's ruler again," Father laughed. "Let's get started." He jammed my hat onto my head.

We headed for the alley that is known as the Devil's Kitchen. There was a different kind of smell to the alley. It was a sweet yet bad kind of smell. We paused at the mouth of the alley. Overhead the moon shone through the bars of the fire escape, and it kept pace with us as we walked inside, like some restless animal pacing in its cage. It was pitch-black in the alley mouth. Without the moonlight, we would have stumbled over the man who lay moaning against the wall.

"Is he—?" I began.

"No," Father said. "Just trying to sleep. If he had any money, he'd be inside."

We turned the corner of the building into a kind of courtyard formed by that building and two others. One gas lamp lit the yard. Father kept his hand on my shoulder. "Keep close to me," he cautioned. We started down the steps into a basement. A bald-headed man perched on a stool behind a counter, his feet inside the rungs. He acted as if he were in some kind of store. He was sipping a cup of tea with one hand while the other rested on his thigh.

The rest of the basement was given over to beds, each of which had a little table beside it. On each table rested a nut-oil lamp, which was used to heat up the pellet of opium before it was put into the long-stemmed pipe. Later, when I went into a demon hospital, it was to remind me very much of a scrubbed-up, antiseptic opium den. On the straw mattresses, men lay in various positions, but of the faces I could see, each of them wore a moronic kind of grin. One man had just put his heated pellet into his pipe. His lips sucked happily at the pipe, which was as long as my arm. Each time he sucked, there was an evil kind of frying sound. The pellet was only good for several lungfuls, but that was enough. The air itself was thick with the smell of opium and with stale sweat and vomit and urine.

The man at the counter put a pellet down on the

counter.

"I'm looking for my cousin," Father said.

The man scratched his forehead with his left little finger. The casual gesture must have actually been some recognition sign. Father scratched the little finger on his right hand.

"You don't look like a brother," the man said.

"I'm not," Father said. "But I once knew men from the Heavenly Order brotherhood. That was back in '97 in the Little City." The Little City was what we called the demons' *Sacramento*, the provincial capital up to the north.

"I hear the fighting was messy," the man behind the counter said. "What did you say your name was?"

"I didn't say." Father looked around the room.

"Well, who are you looking for?"

"A man called Black Dog."

"And he's your cousin?" The man at the counter sat back, satisfied. "So you're the man they call Windrider now."

"Is Black Dog here?"

"No, but I'll send word to your laundry if he does come here." The man gestured toward a teapot. "Have some tea?" he offered, just as if he were in his home.

"No thanks," Father said. "But I'd appreciate that word if he shows up."

"My pleasure," the man said.

As we stepped outside, I turned to Father. "What fighting?"

"Never you mind, boy," Father said.

We went to three other dens, but we had no luck. We were just coming out of the third den when we saw three men appear in the courtyard. Father pressed me back against the door so we were hidden in the shadowed doorway. They walked side by side very deliberately. The two other men who were in the courtyard scuttled out of their way. The sound of the boots echoed hollowly off the walls. The man on the right jerked his head at a basement opium den we had yet to try. "The pig's in there."

"Bring him out," said the man in the middle. Father tightened his hand on my shoulder and he put his finger to his lips, telling me I was to be silent. The man on the right disappeared into the den. There were protests from inside and he reappeared a moment later, half-carrying a man who was naked to the waist. Two men followed him.

"You can't just come breaking into our place like this and taking out one of our customers. You Justices can't push us around even if you are the biggest. There are rules now. Every brotherhood has its own territory—"

The man in the middle held out his right hand. The man on his left lifted up his loose black shirt and pulled out the heavy pistol that he had stuck under his waistband. He handed it to the man in the middle.

The man who had been protesting stopped and dropped to his knees.

"We don't want to start a war with you Bloody Hands, but we will if we have to," said the man in the middle. He nodded at the dopey who had been dragged out of the den. "This pig stole money from one of our foxes. He beat her up, too, so she wouldn't talk."

"So that's how he got all of his money," said the other man from the den. The man on his knees got up and spat at the dopey.

"Take him and good riddance. You can't get any lower than stealing money from a woman." The two men hurried back inside their den. The third Justice propped the dopey up against the railing that ran along the steps to the basement and stepped to one side.

I saw it was Black Dog then. He looked up, confused, studying the three men for a moment until he recognized them. I'll give Black Dog this much. He smiled rather than being afraid. "Lead Hand," Black Dog said to the man in the middle, "I'm going to remember this in the next life and I am going to take definite pleasure in tromping every worm, cockroach, and fly that I meet. I'm sure one of them will be you."

"I never stole any money from any fox," Lead Hand said. "Don't be so sure as to who's going to come back as what." Lead Hand cocked the pistol. You could hear the loud mechanical click. Suddenly I heard a shrill piercing whistle from above me. I looked up to see Father with two fingers in his mouth. He emitted another whistle as I watched. It was a decidedly demonic talent.

I don't think the gunmen would have mistaken Father's whistle for the sound of the police if they had been calm, but of course they were nervous and excited about the killing. The man on Lead Hand's left turned to run, but Lead Hand grabbed his arm. "The gun, you fool, the gun."

Dumbly, the young man let Lead Hand give him the gun. Then the three of them ran like mad for the alleyway.

"Where did you learn to whistle like that?" I asked with open envy.

"Something I picked up," Father said.

"Think you could teach me?"

"Yes, it might just come in handy for you." Father started down the steps three at a time, running toward Black Dog, who lay sprawled across the railing, his legs spread out on the steps. He twisted his head up. He had difficulty focusing his eyes, but finally he recognized Father. "You," he said.

"Yes, me. We've come to take you back to the Company." Father bent over and tried to help Black Dog to his feet, but Black Dog pushed Father's hand away.

"Don't want . . . don't need . . ." Black Dog mumbled.

"Oh, hell," Father said. He swung his fist into Black Dog's jaw with a solid smack. Black Dog sagged on the railing. Father crouched and got Black Dog over his shoulders and walked slowly up the steps. I was waiting for him at the top. "Get his hat and things," Father said.

But I was staring up at Black Dog.

"Remember," Father said, "he was a good man once. Now get his things."

I got Black Dog's hat and shirt and joined Father, who had already started to walk toward the alley mouth.

Chapter 5

Windrider's Claws
(February, 1904–May, 1905)

Later, at the Company, Uncle sat for a long time figuring things on his abacus. The beads clacked as his fingers flew back and forth. Through the ceiling we could hear Black Dog snoring upstairs. "The money can be made up out of my share," Uncle said.

"Don't be an old fool," Father said. "There's not just the matter of the woman to be made up. There's the Justices to be paid off."

"No. Whiskey Devil—he's the head of the Justices—owes me a favor from a long time ago. It won't cost that much."

"Still," White Deer said, "it ought to come out of all our shares. We can write it up to expenses."

"He's my son," Uncle said sternly. "I'm responsible for him."

"Money, money, money," Hand Clap said disgustedly. "Who cares about the money or where it comes from? The point is that any one of us could be a dopey and sleeping upstairs."

Lefty massaged his right arm. "Hand Clap is right. And it would not have to be just dope. It could be gambling for me, or any one of a thousand different traps that a Tang man could fall into in this demons' land."

"Put it to a vote," White Deer said. "All those in favor of sharing the cost, put up your hands." He and Hand Clap put up their hands.

"You're both fools," Uncle began. "Think of your families—"

"They do, old man," Father said. "That's why they're here. But this is their family too. Now will you get talking to your Justices?"

Uncle slammed his abacus down on the table. "Who can talk to fools?" he grumbled, but there was a pleased look in his eye.

As soon as Black Dog had recovered, he promised to reform. He sounded as if he meant it; but then he always did, Hand Clap told me later. Black Dog kept his promise for a time. Pale and shaky, he moved about the laundry working as hard as any of us; but after a while he began to get snappish again, and to sneer at things. It was his way. I think he had lived so long in this land of the demons that his mind had become poisoned and he had begun to think like a demon and to despise the Tang people around him. Maybe when he had first begun to take dope, he had just meant to get away from his conflicts; but after a while, taking dope had become an end in itself.

Now quite a few of the older Tang people used opium. Everybody, including Father, would have an occasional pellet, but that was the way they might have a drink or gamble at the tables. But there were certain individuals who had gone over the edge, who knew no moderation. Opium for Black Dog was what gambling had been for Lefty, but Lefty had stopped, more or less—at least compared to his old days. Black Dog's real problem was his inability to control himself. Finally, one month after we had brought him back, he disappeared. And on the next day, when he came back, we smelled opium's strange, sweet smell—like roasted peanuts—clinging to Black Dog's clothes, and we knew where he had been.

When I had been in the demons' country for over two years, Uncle sent me to make the rounds among some of our regular customers in the Tang people's town to collect overdue bills. As he said, even by demon reckoning it took two figures to write my age, for I was eleven by our system of counting and ten by theirs. I had been collecting money for a month when I saw Black Dog lounging in a doorway, staring at the *May* rain.

"What are you doing here?" I asked.

"I had to take a walk and get some fresh air." He stared up at the sky with a frown and pulled his collar up about his neck. The rain ran down the brim of his hat, splattering on his shoulders. "But it's a miserable day."

"I guess," I said. I had the small canvas bag of money under my loose shirt. "Going back to the Company?"

"Why not?" Black Dog shrugged. He fell into step beside me and we walked up the hill in silence. Black Dog folded his arms across his chest, almost hugging himself. "Don't you . . . don't you hate it here?"

"I don't like it, if that's what you mean, but White Deer says that 'hate' is so strong a word that I ought to use it only for evil."

"But there's another way to forget evil," Black Dog said. We stopped for a moment in a doorway when the rain fell harder.

"Did you ever hear about how we got opium?" he

asked finally.

"The *British* demons forced us to let them sell it in the Middle Kingdom," I said.

"Ah, that's what some people say who want to hide the truth, because they don't want to give the poor man his due. He was a poor working man like you or me who, no matter how hard he worked, always wound up owing more and more to the bosses. The only thing he owned outright was his ugly wife, maybe the ugliest woman alive. She was so repulsive that he beat her in the morning when he got up and beat her in the evening when he came home. The wife never complained, because she loved him dearly. But finally when she saw how much he hated her, she fell ill because she was so sad.

"On her deathbed, she called her husband to her and told him that after her death he would realize how much she loved him despite everything he had done to her. At once the poor farmer felt sorry for what he had done, but before he could tell her, she died. Ten days later, the poor farmer noticed a strange white flower growing from her grave. There was a little round fruit inside the flower. At first the poor farmer was afraid that his wife had turned into some poisonous flower. He could not sleep at night, thinking about the flower and what he had done to his wife. He could not work during the day, remembering the blows he had given her. 'She has every right to hurt me,' the poor farmer said, 'for I have been a mean, spiteful man.'

"With that, he fell sick himself. But he had no money to pay the doctors, nor any offspring to care for him. And then one night during a feverish dream, he saw his wife. She told him that the flower on her grave had been woven from the strands of her soul. The strange fruit in the flower could heal him. He was to cut the fruit and harden the juice that would come out and smoke it. If he smoked it every day, he would become healthy. The very next morning he got up and did as his wife had told him, and no sooner did he take his first puff than he felt his illness leave him. So it was that he and his wife were closer in death than they were in life."

Black Dog smiled ironically. "So it is to those two lovers that I smoke, for the name of the ugly wife was Life and the name of the farmer was Everyman. The only good thing I ever got out of my ugly life was the flower."

I did not understand his story at all. "But life isn't all ugly," I said.

"Don't you think it's ugly here? What kind of lives do we lead without wives and families?"

"There's no money back at home."

"But why sacrifice yourself just so others can get fat at home? All they ever understand is that they need more money."

"Things will be better in the next life. Maybe we'll be born as the sons of noble families. Maybe we'll even finally find release from this world."

Black Dog looked at me intently. "Why shouldn't we get some pleasure in this life? Why later? Why not now?"

"Because we don't owe things just to ourselves. There are others."

He grabbed me by the arm and his voice grew wild. "Don't give me your simpering, mealymouthed answers. We've repaid our debts a dozen times over."

"You're hurting me," I said. All the time, in my mind, I was telling myself that I must not be frightened. I must not be frightened.

"You don't know what pain is," Black Dog said. "Wait till you have been here for thirty years. Then you'll welcome the pain. They were once as pleasant to me as they are to you." He twisted my arm. I let out a yell. I kicked him hard in the knee and he let go of me with a grunt. I began to run up the hill. My hat flew off. I kept on running. I heard his boots come closer as he followed me. Suddenly I felt a pain in the back of my head. He had grabbed my queue. I stopped short as he jerked at the queue, and fell on my back. He tore the money bag away from me, but he did not even look at it. "Pain?" he said strangely. "Pain? You don't know what it is." And he began to kick me with his heavy boots.

When I came to, I was back in the Company. Father was pressing a wet towel against my forehead anxiously. "He's awake," he said. The rest of the Company crowded around me.

"What beast did this to you, boy?" Lefty asked.

I found that I was not even mad at Black Dog. How could you be mad at some dumb, pain-goaded animal? I did not know what to do or say; the Company looked so stern and solemn.

But Uncle took it out of my hands. "Was it Black Dog?" he demanded.

I did not say anything.

"Was it?" Uncle asked.

"Yes," I said reluctantly.

"I'll cut off his head and throw it into the gutter where the dogs can eat it," Uncle said.

"How can you curse your own son that way?" White Deer scolded him.

"He's no son of mine," Uncle declared.

Father turned heavily in his seat. "That's good to know. Then you'll let me take care of him."

"I should have let you or any one of a dozen men take care of him a long time ago. He's not a man. He's an animal," Uncle said.

"You won't do any such thing, Windrider," White Deer said. "Black Dog is a member of the Company."

"Kick him out," Uncle said.

"We'll put it to a vote," White Deer said. "I say bring him to the police and let them handle it."

"Bring him to the demon police?" Uncle asked.

"Yes, the demon police," Lefty said. Hand Clap nodded.

"Otherwise," White Deer reasoned, "you'll have to take it up with the Sleepers. They're not about to let anyone go around beating up one of their brothers without their permission. No matter what he's done."

"The Justices were going to shoot Black Dog," Father pointed out.

"They asked the Sleepers. You ought to know that," Lefty said. "And the Sleepers only gave their permission because they didn't want a war with the Justices."

"I'll go to the Sleepers myself," Uncle said grimly "They won't refuse me permission."

"No," Father let out his breath in a rush. "No. I'm sick of having to deal with thieves and pimps and pushers. I'm sick of having to scrape and bow to men who live off the misery of their brothers and sisters."

"Now, now," White Deer soothed. "There are many good men in the brotherhoods who earn their money as we do and who don't deal with those things. It's only a small number who are criminals."

But Father whirled around to face White Deer. "Don't you see? We're all tainted by it. As long as we keep quiet and let it go on, we're as bad as they are. It eats at them; it eats at us."

The others were silent. Father might have slapped

each one of them in the face. He should have kept his mouth shut then, but the dragon-ness in him would not let him. He had to speak his mind. "We mustn't play their games anymore by their rules."

"They are our brothers," Uncle said, "no matter how bad. That's why we don't go to the demon police. We Tang people take care of our own affairs. It's better that way. Remember the virtues of the Stranger, the lonely man in foreign lands: Be silent; be cunning; be invisible. Besides, what's the use of going to the demons? The Sleepers can afford to pay more bribes to the police than we can. The demons will just listen to our complaint and then file it away. Better to go to the Sleepers themselves."

"If you won't go to the demons, there's only one other way to make sure that justice is done," Father said. "And that's to do it myself." There was something about his posture and the look of his eye that reminded me of dragons. All the others in the room could feel it too.

Then I realized that to be a dragon meant more than just taking an interest in the magic of machines. It was also to live by the spirit of dragons, and Father felt that no dragon would let such an act go unpunished.

"Dragons," Father went on, "protect their own brood."

"Dragons, dragons, dragons. Always that nonsense," Uncle said impatiently. I think he instantly regretted his words, for Father's mouth hardened at that.

Father sat back in his chair. It creaked under the shift of weight. "When I was there on the beach and in the dragon kingdom, it was more real a time than this."

"Don't kill yourself for a foolish dream," Uncle

insisted. He would not have said such cruel things normally, but he was worried about Father. "And besides you promised . . ." He glanced at me and was quiet.

"What promise?" I asked.

It was a long time before Father spoke. He folded his hands and looked at them while he talked. "You do many strange things when you're young. And maybe the strangest thing you do is join a secret society that says it's dedicated to throwing out the Manchus. You enlist. You act as a soldier for the future of the Middle Kingdom. And then you realize that though they make a lot of patriotic speeches, at heart they're only criminals."

"And did you do that?"

"I once was a Sleeper," Father said. The others left our room shortly after that. But we no sooner had turned off the gaslight and lain down than we heard a bump at the door. Father got up and opened it, to see Lefty sitting in the hallway facing our door. The hallway was so narrow that though Lefty had his back against the wall, he had to draw his knees up toward his chest. By his left side he had a club.

He smiled apologetically. "Excuse me, Windrider. I meant to be quiet. Hand Clap should never have eaten so much squash. That one has so much gas that I cannot stand sleeping in the same room with him, so I have come out here for cleaner air."

"Right by my door?"

"The air is cleaner here."

Father slammed the door shut.

"Why should the air be cleaner here?" I asked him.

"Be quiet," Father snapped. "The fools are trying to keep me in." We had no window in our room, so the only way out was through the door. Father paced around the room. Finally he seemed to notice me again. "Go to sleep, Shadow."

"How do you expect to be reborn again as a dragon if you act like a criminal?" I asked him.

"Dragons have claws, too." Father pushed me down on the mat and drew the quilt up about my neck. "Now go to sleep."

I felt rather than heard Father stir. He lit the gaslight, keeping it dim. Half awake, I watched as he rolled off his mat and got dressed, except for his boots. Then he went to our trunk and eased the lid up, piling the things silently on the floor until he reached the very bottom. From this he drew a flat rectangular package, and he undid the plain cotton cloth about it. The demons called it a hatchet, but it was really a squarish sword, looking much like a cleaver except that the balance was truer. The light gleamed on the blade. He set it down by the door.

Then he found his boots and set them down by his sword. He put his hand on the doorknob and leaned his ear against the door as if listening to Lefty in the hallway. Father straightened, and wriggled his shoulders as if to relax them. He took several deep breaths before he jerked the door open.

I had never seen Father move so fast. He jerked the door open, and Lefty had time to stare up in disbelief as he groped for his club when Father's fist hit him in the jaw. Lefty's head tilted back sharply and he had a glassy look in his eyes. As he began to slump over, Father caught him and eased him to the floor.

I closed my eyes quickly when Father came back into our room. I raised my eyelids slightly so I could watch Father pick up his hat, boots, and sword in one hand before he closed the door. I remembered again that Mother had told me to look after Father. I scrambled for my things, and with my boots clutched against my chest I padded after him. I was just in time to see him pull on his boots before he went outside.

I counted to ten before I followed him outside. It was a night when the thick fog drifted through the streets and I could not see more than an arm's length before me, and everything seemed unreal, as if I were asleep and dreaming. The gaslights showed in the fog only as dull spots of light—like ghosts hovering. A building would appear out of the grayness and then disappear. The whole world seemed to have become unglued. If ever there was a night for monsters to be out, this was the night.

I could hear Father's steady, determined bootsteps fading away into the distance. I decided not to put my boots on after all, because the echoes might tell Father I was behind him. I shivered as I walked on the cold, wet pavement. I picked my way through the garbage and over the occasional demon who lay sprawled on the street with the vacant look of a dopey. We went two blocks down *Dupont Street,* and then one block up the steep Street of the Tang People, into an alley. I crept down the alley until I dimly saw Father's tall figure bulk out of the mist. He knocked at a door. I ducked into a nearby doorway.

"Who is it?" a voice asked.

"It's the Windrider. I want to see the Water Fairy."

"Who?"

"Some call him the Tiger General now."

The little door shut, and Father stood unmoving there in the cold, his collar turned up, his sword in one hand. I stood shivering, my boots clutched to my chest, afraid to go to him but afraid to leave. I knew that the Tiger General was the head of the brotherhood, but how he had gotten that other name—as improbable as it sounded—I did not know.

Finally the door opened and I saw a small, wizened man. "It's been a long time since anyone used that name."

"My Uncle has a long memory, reaching back to the railroad camps and a young man who drank the water as the demons did without boiling it first. He told all the other Tang people what a superior stomach he had. He took sick with the cramps and the runs."

"That name is the only thing that saved you from being shot down on our doorstep. I wanted to see what fool would dare to use it. I should have known it would be you."

"All that's past. Send my kinsman out to me."

But the Tiger General stayed where he was. "It's in my mind that you and Black Dog may have been mortal enemies in some former lives and done great harm to one another. You never did get along, from the day you joined us to the day you quit."

"Think what you like." Father shrugged. "But I beg you to keep this matter between the two of us."

While the two talked, I had watched a shadow creep out of the narrow alley between the Sleepers' hall and the building I was in. The shadow ducked back into the alley mouth. In his hand was a heavy pistol.

"He beat up my son the money he had collected," Father said. "Do you protect child beaters and thieves?"

The Tiger General considered that for a moment and then turned in the doorway. "Tell our brother that he has a caller." There was scuffling from within. Then the Tiger General stepped aside as Black Dog was pushed, stumbling, out into the street. He paused for a moment, on all fours. His shirt was rumpled as if he had been dragged to the door. He stood up and smoothed out his shirt.

"I'm sick. A dopey is always sick," he said to Father.

"You weren't too sick to beat up my boy. Now fight," Father said.

"But you're armed, and as you can see . . ." Black Dog held up his empty hands. One of his brothers tossed a sword out onto the cobblestones. Black Dog turned to look with astonishment at the others. The Tiger General merely folded his hands behind his back.

Reluctantly, Black Dog bent slowly, as if his back hurt. "Now," he shouted and straightened quickly, raising the sword over his head to throw it. The man in the alley stepped out, cocking his pistol. He began to aim at Father. I threw myself against the man— literally threw my whole body, as if it were only an object, against him. I hit him in the stomach and he collapsed with a grunt. To my astonishment, I found I still held my boots. I began to use the heavy-soled boots like clubs, flailing at the man.

Black Dog cut viciously at Father's head, but Father had accurately judged the length of Black Dog's swing and kept his head just an inch out of the reach of the sword, using his own body to draw Black Dog's swings. It was as if Father were playing with him. Panting, Black Dog cut again and again at Father's head, but he always just missed. Panicked, Black Dog tried one huge, powerful cut and missed. He missed on his back swing too. Then Father had cut Black Dog across the chest, laying open the shirt. Black Dog stumbled and fell back with a shout.

An arm caught me across the chest and I was tossed off by the man. My head hit the cobblestones hard and I lay there, looking up breathlessly at a man in his forties. In his hand was the pistol and it was aimed at me. Then suddenly the man jerked his head back and he twitched. There was the sound of a meaty smack and he fell face forward across my legs, Father's sword in his back. Father picked up the man's pistol and whirled.

The Tiger General and some of the brothers had stepped onto the sidewalk. The Tiger General held up his hands apologetically. "It was supposed to be between just you and Black Dog."

"And now?"

The Tiger General prodded the dead man in the leg. "It is still between you and Black Dog for all we care." He turned to one of the brothers. "Bind up Black Dog's wound and gather his things. He is no longer a member of this brotherhood. I have had enough of his disobedience. He's already been warned of the penalty." The Tiger General turned back to us. "Are you satisfied?"

"Is he?" Father jerked his head in Black Dog's direction.

"I cannot say." The Tiger General shrugged. "But now when you settle this matter later, it will be strictly a private affair."

I slid out from underneath the dead man, staring at his blood that had spattered my pants leg. Father jerked his sword free from the man's back and wiped the blade carefully on the shirt of the dead man. "Put your boots on, Moon Shadow."

Father stood up and turned back again to the Tiger General. "The Company wasn't responsible. I acted on my own."

The Tiger General crossed his arms across his chest. "You'd best get out of our town for a while. Not that I care for the likes of those two pigs, but there are some brothers who would resent the death of a brother, no matter what kind of a fool he was."

"I understand," Father said.

Father put me to bed and then began to write a letter. I was so sleepy that I fell asleep before I could ask him why he was writing it then. The next morning Father left early, while I was still asleep. When I woke up, nobody knew where he had gone. He did not come back until around noon, when he walked solemnly over to Uncle. "I have already written my wife and mother telling them about the trouble last night. I have told them we have to leave the Tang people's town."

Uncle put down the pair of trousers he had been washing. The steam in the laundry had slicked his hair down against his face. "Where will you go?"

"Out there among the demons," Father said.

"Don't be a fool. There is nothing that money can't fix—even the killing of a brother," Uncle snapped. "What can you do out there?"

"I went to see a demon, a *Mister Alger,* who manages apartment houses. I have a job, cleaning and fixing things in those houses. I can heal sick machines on the side too."

"And where will you live then?" Uncle demanded. "What demon would rent to you?"

"There is one demoness. She was once rich but now she's poor. She lets people live in her house for money. They have a stable that they converted into a little room. I'll stay there with my boy."

"You can speak their tongue well enough to collect bills, but not well enough to live among them."

"I can speak the language of machines," Father said. "That will get us by."

"To hear you talk, you'd think it was you who'd been knocked on the head instead of your boy."

"Maybe I have been," Father said. "I feel like I've just woken from some long dream. I can follow the dragons' ways better among the demons than among the Tang people."

"That's the real reason," Uncle snapped. "But don't you understand me? It's dangerous out there for a Tang man. Just the other day some demon boys caught Melon Head in the street. Now he's blind in one eye. And that was just traveling from the ferry into the Tang people's town. He wasn't even trying to live among them."

"We won't ever have to travel very far away from our home. We ought to be safe."

Uncle waved his hand. "Then go, and good riddance to a fool." He was hurt and angry and afraid for us all at the same time. I don't think he could really understand why any Tang people would want to leave the safety of our town to live among the demons. I suppose it would have been possible to go on living near the Sleepers, but it would have meant paying an expensive compensation to them— money Father did not want to pay. And then, too, I think he truly believed that he could follow the dragon-ness within him better among the demons. The fact that he was willing to live among the demons was a measure of how strongly he believed.

Despite Father's words, he seemed as sad as I was the next day when we left the Company. He had gone in the morning to clean up our new home. When he came back in the afternoon, we got ready to go. Uncle stayed upstairs in his room while we loaded our possessions into the Company's delivery wagon. And then, when the very last box of wires and parts and tools had been loaded into the wagon,

Father went up for one last visit to our room. I had stayed downstairs out of courtesy to him. Then the Company gathered around us when Father came back down.

There were presents, of course. White Deer gave us a little statue of the Buddha-to-be, a happy, laughing god who would exist in the future when all mankind had been liberated from the material world. Lefty gave us his magnificently written poem which he could never reduplicate because he had lost his hand. Hand Clap gave each of us a little charm on a necklace. On the charm was inscribed the name of the Demon Stomper, who was most often portrayed as a man in a tattered robe sticking a knife into one eye of a demon while he pulled out the other. It had been blessed by priests back home—the Enlighteners, they were called, because their monastery was the Place of Full Enlightenment. Everyone was impressed by Hand Clap's gift.

And then we heard the sound of a door slamming upstairs and footsteps. Uncle had on his best outfit, looking as splendid as any lord. His arms were folded across his stomach and his hands were hidden in the great sleeves. He hid his affection behind his gruffness. "Well, you young fool, are you finally finished making enough racket to tear down the house?"

"Yes, Uncle," Father said quietly.

Suddenly Uncle took a porcelain cup from his sleeve. There was a little bit of dark soil in it. In his other hand, he held some incense sticks. "Here," he said.

There is no way of identifying dirt, of course, but we all knew it must come from Uncle's own little cup of soil that he had brought back after one of his trips to home. For Uncle the soil was very special, being a bit of the Middle Kingdom and home, and more: part of the land which his fathers and their fathers had worked before him.

"Put it in front of all your gods and your demon toys and burn some incense in it."

Father cleared his throat. "Thank you."

"Here, here," Uncle said in an annoyed voice. He thrust the cup and incense sticks into my hands. His own hands disappeared inside his sleeves again. "And good riddance to you."

He would have turned away, but Father on impulse suddenly stuck out his hand. Uncle stared at it for a moment and then, like a demon, took it and shook hands with Father. Then Father shook hands like a demon with all the others, rather than bowing and saying good-bye. He was determined to begin doing things in the demonic fashion.

We mounted the buckboard next to Hand Clap. I sat between him and Father. Then Father cracked the reins on the backside of Red Rabbit, and with a lurch the wagon set off. I held the cup in my hands, looking at the familiar buildings passing by. Oh, I would be back to shop for things. Father thought it more prudent if I did the shopping in the Tang people's town for a while. But it would not be the same. Most of my day would be spent away from here.

I felt Father's hand on my shoulder. He nodded at the cup. "We'll give that a special place," he said kindly.

Chapter **6**

The Demoness
(May, 1905)

In those days *Polk Street* was for the poorer demons. There were lots of common little shops like grocery stores or poultry markets and wooden tenement houses, some four stories high, into which the poor demons crowded. In the morning you would see the demons in undershirts and coats, swinging lunch buckets as they walked to the factories, and the demonesses hurrying to be on time in the rich mansions one block to the west, where they worked as laundresses or housekeepers or housemaids. There would be young demons who were clerks in offices, tugging at their stiff celluloid collars as they ran to catch the *cable cars,* and shopgirls in their long dresses walking in groups, talking in excited voices.

All day the streets would be filled with noise: the sound of the hooves of the great dray horses as they clopped up and down the cobblestones and the merry ringing of the *cable cars* on the streets that crossed *Polk.* The demonesses might be back later in the day, pushing baby carriages or walking with their employers' wives, doing the day's shopping. And in the later afternoon, everyone would come home, looking tired, hardly noticing the demons who lit the gas lamps.

I had been through streets like *Polk Street* before, when we had picked up laundry, but we had only been passing through then. Now we were here to stay. The tenement houses had the same odd, flat faces and the same drab colors, making them look all the same, as if they had been hatched in the same brood. Their doorways gaped like mouths and their windows gleamed like eyes, so that each one of them looked like the stark, empty face of a multi-eyed demon.

We stopped finally in front of a neat little Victorian house with an odd shape. It seemed to have a little more character than the tenement houses. I found out later that it had eight sides instead of being built in the shape of a square. The demon who had built the house had wanted it that way. Actually, it made that house seem all the more scary, because behind its iron fence, it looked like some strange beast that had to be kept specially separate and fenced off from the others. It squatted there like some toad made of glass and wood and shingles. In one corner was a turret with a big bay window looking out on a small garden surrounded by the fence.

"Here we are," Father said. He picked me up and swung me down to the sidewalk. "You watch our things," he added. I watched uncomfortably as he and Hand Clap each grabbed a box of our belongings and walked into the alley between the iron fence of the house and the tenement next door. When they disappeared from sight, I wasn't sure what to do. On the one hand, I was supposed to watch our boxes; but on the other hand, I didn't want to be alone. I walked cautiously toward the mouth of the alley, but I couldn't see Father.

It seemed to me at that time that there might be any number of demons waiting in their houses, waiting patiently for me to turn my back so they could leap upon me and take over my body, or torture me, or do the hundred and one things that demons can do to people. I looked up at that moment and saw a pink demonic face staring down at me from the glass eye of the turret. When it saw me looking, it vanished. I ran back to the wagon. I stayed there all the time, clinging to the familiar shape of the Company's wagon while Father and Hand Clap unloaded our things. It did not take long, since we did not have very much.

Hand Clap sat on the seat of the wagon for a moment, the reins in his hand but reluctant to tell Red Rabbit to go. We were just as reluctant. We stood on the sidewalk beside the wagon. My hand held on to the side. For want of something to do, Hand Clap scratched his neck and looked around. Then he began to sniff the air. "There's money to be made here by a man with the know-how," he said. "I can just smell the gold coins piled in all these houses, and I can just see all these poor demons sitting on top of their heaps of gold, crying because their clock's busted and they don't know how to fix it. They'll be mobbing your place day and night to fix things once they know you're here."

Father laughed. "Careful, or some jealous demon will wish us bad luck."

Hand Clap sat back in the seat. "With that charm I gave you? Listen, if some dumb demon is too ignorant to recognize its power and comes a-knocking at your door, why, you tell me and I'll tell the Enlighteners, and they'll come flying across the ocean and gobble that demon up from the top of his hair down to his big ugly feet."

"You do that." Father slapped Hand Clap's leg. "Now you'd better be going. Red Rabbit looks hungry."

"He's always hungry," Hand Clap said.

"Remember though," I said, "he likes a carrot in the morning."

"I'll remember." Hand Clap nodded a good-bye to Father and winked at me. Then he shook the reins, but Red Rabbit would not leave. He looked around at Father as if telling him to get back on the wagon.

"Go on, you fat, overgrown, sassy rabbit," Hand Clap ordered as he shook the reins, but Red Rabbit stubbornly stayed put.

"Get out of here before I skin you and make a jacket out of your hide," Father said. With his hat, he whacked Red Rabbit's rump real good. With a snort of hurt pride, Red Rabbit started in his harness; but then he stayed put.

"Go on," Father said, and he whacked Red Rabbit even harder.

With a sad twist of his head, Red Rabbit turned away from Father and began to clop along in his slow, methodical pace. From the way he went, you might have thought he was pulling a ton of metal instead of an empty wagon. Together we watched them roll down the cobblestone street and turn the corner.

"Come along." Father put his hand on my shoulder and steered me around to face the alley. We walked past the iron fence and the garden to a big back yard that was filled with trees and grass. A stable stood in one corner of the yard. Father swung the door open. It creaked on its hinges, and I could smell the disinfectant Father had used to clean out the stable that morning.

In one corner of the room was a potbellied stove with a pipe leading up to the ceiling. Our mats and blankets were laid in one corner. Boards had been propped against one wall for the day when Father would build shelves. Until that time, our stuff would stay in our boxes. I wandered around the room and touched everything to reassure myself that it was real and not some demonic illusion. Father waited patiently in the doorway with his arms folded. When I went back to him, I nodded that it was all right. He grinned.

The first thing he did was to put up a shelf. Then he set Monkey and the Buddha-to-be on it. He placed the cup of soil before them and stuck some incense sticks into the soil and lit them, so that Monkey and the Buddha-to-be would be comfortable in the pleasant smoke. Finally Father nodded his head in the direction of the house. "Now we have to meet our landlady. Her name is *Miss Whitlaw.*"

"*Miss Whitlaw.*" I practiced the syllables several times until Father sighed. "That will have to do for now." Then he spat into his hand and smoothed back my hair. He frowned. "How do you ever manage to get so dirty?"

"I washed my face this morning like you told me."

"Not very well," he said. He picked up an empty pail and went outside. I watched from the doorway as he worked the pump handle until the water splashed into the pail. He came back inside and got some clean hand towels. He threw me one. "Now wash," he said.

"You'd think," I grumbled, "that we were visiting the Empress herself."

Father wet his towel in the pail and began to wash his face. "Your mother was always polite to everyone. She always said that you never knew if that person might have been some king or queen in a former life."

"But these are white demons," I protested.

Father opened our trunk and got out some clean, well-ironed shirts—some of White Deer's masterpieces. "You can take that up with your mother when she comes here herself. Until then, we'll do as she says. Understand?"

I said nothing because I was still annoyed, but I rubbed my face vigorously anyway—in fact harder than Mother used to do it. I was not going to be accused of being unfaithful.

When I had changed into my clean shirt, Father announced we were ready. Finally we stepped outside. Standing there in that empty back yard, I was afraid, and then I thought of the Old Ones. Perhaps they were watching. I had to try to act brave at least.

Father took my hand as if he knew I needed the support, and we started toward the demon house. On the way he pointed to the outhouse that sat at the end of the dirt lot. Then we went up the back steps and knocked at the door. Under my shirt, I wore the charm to keep demons away.

I think that the demoness had been waiting for us, because Father had no sooner knocked once than she opened the door. She was the first demoness that I had ever seen this close up, and I stared. I had expected her to be ten feet tall with blue skin and to have a face covered with warts and ear lobes that hung all the way down to her knees so that her ear lobes would bounce off the knees when she walked. And she might have a potbelly shiny as a mirror, and big sacs of flesh for breasts, and maybe she would only be wearing a loin cloth.

Instead I saw a petite lady, not much bigger than Hand Clap. She had a large nose—but not absurdly so—and a red face and silver hair; and she wore a long dress of what looked like white cotton, over which she had put a red apron. The dress was freshly starched, and crinkled when she moved and smelled good. She had a smile like the Listener, She Who Hears Prayers, who refused release from the cycle of lives until all her brothers and sisters too could be freed from sin.

"*Well,*" she said. "*Well.*" I looked at her eyes and saw a friendly twinkle in them that made her seem even less threatening. There were demons, after all, who could be kindly disposed. I suddenly felt calm and unafraid as I stood before her.

My father nudged me. I bowed carefully and presented our present. It was a paper picture of the Stove King, who reported to the Lord of Heaven each year about what the family had done—both the good things and the bad things. It was customary each New Year's to bribe the little Stove King. Some families offered him cookies and tea, which he could snack on during his journey to heaven. Others took a more direct approach and smeared his face with honey. Still others bought little paper horses and carts so he could ride up to heaven in style. After all these centuries of tender loving care from millions of Tang families, the Stove King had gotten quite pudgy. Father thought it might be a nice gesture to give the picture to the demoness and I agreed, for the little Stove King might take the demons' ignorance into account and give a good report for them; for the Stove King was basically as kind and gentle a person as one was likely to find among the gods.

The demoness turned it over and over in her hands in puzzlement until Father spoke. "*He Chinee saint of kitchen."* I doubt if the demoness would have had a "heathen" god inside her kitchen but a holy man was a different matter.

"Well, isn't that nice." She smiled pleasantly and stepped aside from the door. *"Please, do come in."*

We sat down at a table covered with a cheery red-checkered tablecloth in a cold, abstract arrangement of squares—the kind of pattern the demons favored.

And of course all the smells to her kitchen were different. The demoness went to her icebox—a strange device—and took out a pitcher and poured a large glass of some white liquid for me. For herself and for Father, she made tea, using water from a copper teakettle that she must have already boiled and set at the edge of the stove to keep hot. Then the demoness set down the biggest plate of things before me. They were brown-colored and shaped like men, and icing had been used to make eyes, noses, and button coats.

"They're"—it sounded like—*"jin-jer-ber-ed cookies,"* she said.

I looked to Father to explain the demonic word which I did not know.

"Gin-ger-bread," Father said slowly. "It's a kind of sweet ginger-flavored cookie or cake."

"And what's this stuff?" I looked dubiously at the glass of thick, white liquid.

"Cow's milk."

I almost made a face but caught myself. "But that's cow urine."

"No, no, stupid. Milk comes from the cow's udders. Now drink it. You must not offend the lady."

I glanced at the demoness. She smiled at me. It was nice of her to think of me as a demon child—I guess. I sipped the liquid and managed not to make a face at the awful, greasy taste.

"Go on and have a cookie," Father ordered me sternly. "And you better eat all of it."

The milk did not make me inclined to trust the demoness' cookies much. "They look like dung," I said.

"I don't care if it is dung. She made it. You eat it."

"I will if you will."

Father sighed. He turned to the demoness. *"May I?"*

"Certainly," she said with a gracious smile.

Father took one of the cookies and munched at it. Well, he did not change into a toad or anything; and he did not throw up—I had been expecting either possibility. I tried one of the cookies on the plate before me. The taste was heavenly. I gobbled up one and started for another.

"Hey," Father snapped. "First you don't want any. Now you want to gobble them all up like a pig."

"Go on." The demoness pushed the plate closer to me. She smiled in real pleasure. I suddenly liked the way all the wrinkles in her face crinkled up in tiny smiles. I had another cookie. And then I was so thirsty that even the white stuff did not taste so bad this time.

Father and the demoness talked politely about the neighborhood—where was the best place to shop for what. The demoness seemed genuinely to want to help us, and I began to think that she was one of the good demons. I looked about her kitchen—curiosity got the better of politeness. When I finally finished looking around her kitchen, I realized I had gone through four more of the cookies.

Father noticed the almost empty plate at the same time. *"Look at this boy,"* he said in exasperation. *"He eat enough for four pigs."* He started to apologize to the demoness, but she only smiled prettily again.

"There's only one real compliment for a cook, and that's for her guests to eat everything up. You must take the rest of the cookies with you." She smoothed her apron over her lap and winked at me secretly.

"You too kind." Father spread his hands. *"You make us ashame."* He kicked me gently under the table.

"Yes, ashame," I piped up.

At that moment I heard a crash and the kitchen door swung open, and there was a demon girl about my age lying on her stomach. She must have been listening at the door and lost her balance. It was only later that I realized her face was not always a bright red, but was only that way when she was angry or perhaps embarrassed. The demoness jumped up and slapped her hand to her forehead.

"Oh, that child," she said. *"She'll be the death of me yet. You, Robin. I told you not to spy on our new guests."*

"You said I wasn't to look," the demon girl said as she got up, dusting herself off. *"You didn't say anything about listening."*

Father hid a smile as the demoness let out a little sigh. *"Well, the harm's been done. Let me introduce you."* She turned around with an apologetic smile. *"This is my niece, Robin. When my brother and sister-in-law died, I took her in."*

"Auntie calls me her burden," the demon girl added.

"I call you my treasure, too." The demoness slipped her arm around the demon girl and held her against her side. *"Though not very often, I'll admit."*

Father stood up and bowed. He poked me and I slid off the chair and did the same. I did not mean to be rude when I stared at her, but she was the first demon child I had seen this close. For all I knew, demon children were not like me, but like dolls or toys that the demons took out of boxes for a while to decorate their sidewalks and then stored away again inside their homes.

The demon girl was like and unlike what I imagined one of them to be. She seemed like a dwarf copy of her aunt, and her red face looked like a lantern that had been filled with blood and was going to burst at any moment. Her hair was the strangest color golden-red—as though her head had just burst into flame. She wore a short dress that I recognized as *gingham*, and her knees and legs had many scratches and scars on them.

And then I saw something in the demon girl's hand. It was a long rod with lenses at one end and a card, with two pictures on it, held in a rack at the other. The demoness saw the direction in which I was looking. *"Show* Moon Shadow *our stereopticon, Robin."*

The demon girl held the device up to her face so the lenses were against her eyes. *"You look through it like this,"* she said. *"Here, you try it."*

I put the viewer to my eyes and almost gasped, for it seemed as if I were suddenly in another world and no longer in the kitchen. Huge falls thundered right before me.

"That's Niagara Falls," the demon girl said.

Later it was explained to me that each eye sees the same object from a slightly different angle, so that each eye has a slightly different picture. It's the brain that combines the two pictures together into one image and creates the stereoptical effect: the depth that the world seems to have for us. The *stereopticon* card has two pictures of the same object, but each picture is taken from a slightly different angle. Each of the viewer's eyes focuses on one of the pictures and the brain, in trying to put them together, gives the viewer the illusion of depth as if he were not looking at two pictures on a flat card, but rather as if he were looking at the real thing. Of course, at that moment, I did not know all this, so I was very impressed.

Father looked through it for a long time. "Dragon magic?" I asked him.

"It's magic of the mind, if not of the dragons," Father said. He handed it back to the demon girl, pleased and surprised. *"It . . . it . . . fun."* He struggled for the right words and could not find them.

"Yes, Mr. Lee," the demoness said with a faint smile. *"We travel all the way around the world with it and yet never leave our parlor. We have more cards. Would you like to see them?"*

"Oh, yes," Father said.

She led us out of the kitchen into a hallway smelling of polish and old wood, and then into a carpeted room with a bird inside a glass jar and books stacked neatly in a bookcase to one side. Later, I learned that most of them were travel books. The demoness and the demon girl would go to almost any lecturer who was giving a *magic lantern* show with *slides* of his travels. The demoness' father had never really had any time to take her traveling, which was too bad, since she loved to travel.

But as the demon girl fetched the box of viewing cards, I was looking at one corner of the room that was filled with a blend of strange colors. I looked up to see that it was the result of a window.

"Would you like to see our stained-glass window?" the demoness asked gently.

I glanced at Father and he nodded, so I walked

over to it until I was about two yards away.

"*You can take a closer look than that,*" the demoness said.

It was a tall, rectangular window. On the outside there was a border of flowers and vines made from bits of colored glass set into a lead frame. But on the inner part of the window there was a great green creature, breathing yellow and red flames and biting at the spear that a silver-clad demon thrust into him.

With a rustle of skirts, the demoness joined me.

"*What's that?*" I asked, pointing at the green creature.

"*A dragon,*" she said. "*You know. It's a very wicked animal that breathes fire and goes about eating up people and destroying towns. St. George killed many of them.*"

I looked at Father horrified, for these demons had turned the story of dragons upside down if they thought a holy man would kill them. But Father answered for me. "*Very interesting. We have dragons too.*"

"*Do you have a Chinese saint who did the same things as St. George?*" the demoness asked with obvious satisfaction.

"You should tell them the truth about dragons," I told Father.

"Maybe dragons in the demon lands are all as evil as they believe." Father shrugged. "At any rate, when you're someone's guest, you don't correct her no matter how wrong she may be."

The demoness had waited patiently during this exchange. Now she asked, "*What did he say?*"

"*My boy, he ask if you make,*" Father lied.

"*Oh, no. Papa had the window brought from England.*" She lovingly traced the curves of part of the lead frame. "*Papa said no home was complete without a stained-glass window.*" And in my heart, I agreed with her, for it was a lovely thing even if the scene it depicted was all wrong. The demoness added, *"Papa also said that no one owned a stained-glass window. It was meant to be shared—so you feel free to come look through it any time you want, Moon Shadow."*

"You too kind."

"Fiddlesticks," Miss Whitlaw said.

In the meantime, Robin had sat down on a bench before a boxlike contraption taller than her and made of black wood. She lifted up a kind of lid about halfway down on its front, exposing thin white and black tiles of ivory. She began poking at the tiles aimlessly, producing strange musical sounds.

"What's that?" I asked Father.

"The demons call it an *upright piano,*" Father said.

Miss Whitlaw must have recognized the last two words. *"Robin plays it very well."*

"Oh, but you play so much better, Auntie," Robin said.

"Now, Robin," Miss Whitlaw said, *"I don't think they want to hear an old lady's antiquated repertory."*

"Please, we not hear before." Father poked me in the side.

"Yes, please," I chimed in.

Robin left the bench as Miss Whitlaw came over. She smoothed her long skirt underneath her and sat down with a little flounce like a young girl. She was smiling in a pleased but embarrassed manner. She turned to her niece. *"What should I play, Robin?"*

Robin was standing beside the *upright piano.* *"Play 'Simple Gifts,' Auntie."*

Miss Whitlaw inclined her head to one side. *"Well, all right."*

Her fingers moved over the tiles, drawing deep

resonant sounds from within the big box, and she began to sing in a high, sweet voice.

We did not follow too many of the words then, but the demoness played it and Robin sang it so often that I eventually got them:

'Tis the gift to be simple;
'Tis the gift to be free,
'Tis the gift to come down
Where you ought to be.

And when we find ourselves
In the place just right
'Twill be in the valley
Of love and delight.

When true simplicity is gained,
To bow and to bend,
We shan't be ashamed.
To turn, turn,
Will be our delight,
Till by turning, turning,
We come round right.

And just then, the late sun must have shone on this side of the building. The dragon suddenly stood out in luminous greens and yellows and reds, and I thought to myself, if there is light that comes from the magical pearl in the dragon's forehead, then it must be like the light of this window. The shafts of colored light shot across the room to where the demoness sat. Her skirt seemed to gather in a distorted picture of the dragon in the window—or not really distorted, but an image that was alive. For the glass had been cast unevenly, so that there were odd little flamelike curves in the colors. The image seemed to be so full of life, in fact, that it was bursting out of its outline.

And I thought to myself, Mother must be right. The kind of person who would own such a window must surely have been royalty in some other life. I found myself wishing more than ever that Mother could be with me right then. I was sure she would agree with me. Later, as I got to know the demoness, I was to realize that despite her demonic appearance and dress and speech and customs, there was a gentle strength, a sweet loving patience coupled with an iron-hard core of what she thought was right and proper. I was always to think of her as the demoness who kept the dragon fire locked inside a window.

After the song, the demoness spoke some more about dragons and I began to feel sorry for her. Her dragons were sly, spiteful creatures who stole people's gold and killed people for malicious fun. They sounded more and more like what Mother and Grandmother had told me about the outlaw dragons. It was a shame that the demoness had not gotten to know the true dragons of the sea, who were wise and benevolent.

But Father only smiled when I told him that, later when we were back in our stable. "You know how the demons are," he said. "They turn everything upside down and get everything the wrong way."

As I helped Father tug off his boots, I asked him something else that had been bothering me. "Do you think the demoness is the ghost of a Tang woman? I mean she could have forgotten a lot even if she was a ghost."

Father grunted as one boot came off. "Maybe. Maybe not."

I began to work off his other boot. "Or do you think the demoness might have been some Tang woman who did something so terrible in a former life that she was reborn here as a white demoness?"

When the boot came off in my hands, Father massaged his feet. "Maybe that, too."

"I don't think she can be a ghost," I decided finally.

"I never heard of a ghost banished from the Middle Kingdom and made to forget so many things. But then she must have done something pretty bad if she was reborn over here as a demoness instead of back in the Middle Kingdom at least as some kind of animal."

Father tousled my hair. "You think too much."

As I lay down on my mat and pulled the blanket up about my neck, it seemed to me that if this was the case, the demoness would surely be reborn as a rich Tang woman in her next life. I even toyed with the idea that perhaps we had been close to each other in some former life—a mother and child, even. If that were so, I at least owed it to her to set her straight on dragons. It was with these thoughts that I fell asleep.

Chapter 7

Educations
(May–June, 1905)

The next day was much like every day for me during our stay among the demons. I got up just before dawn and got the fire going in the stove and put water on to boil and cooked our morning rice. I would help Father with his handyman chores in certain of *Mr. Alger's* buildings that were in safe areas. Father said it ought to be all right to do my shopping anytime from the morning to the early afternoon, because there were mostly harmless shoppers on the streets then. But I had to be back at the stable before the demon children got out of school. I was also to avoid any demons or demonesses standing about in large groups talking idly. I followed Father's orders faithfully. I had no desire to get beaten up or strung from a lamppost by my hair. In the evening, after I had cooked dinner and washed up, there would be lessons in reading and writing the Tang people's words and in the use of the abacus for arithmetic. I lived my life like that every day except for the demons' seventh day, *Sunday.*

As you can see, this did not leave me much time to

follow my original program of reeducating the demoness about dragons. But despite everything, Father made it a point to let me have half an hour free each day. I could do anything I wanted during that time: spit at the walls, sleep on my mat, or simply go off on my own. I think Father was secretly pleased when, a few days after we moved in, I decided to use the time to pay another visit to the demoness.

I don't mean to make myself sound like a goody-goody. She was a demoness to me at that time, who lived in a magical kind of lair. It was an adventure. It was a challenge. And if I could remind her of some of the true things about dragons that people ought to know but that she seemed to have forgotten, well, that was to the good. I went up to the demoness' house in my clean tunic and pants, my boots shined and my face scrubbed—and my charm around my neck. She smiled quietly and prettily as she had that first day.

"*Why, come in*, Moon Shadow." Miss Whitlaw stood away from the door. "*Would you like some cookies and milk?*"

"*Maybe cookies and tea?*" I asked. I held up the small package I had brought. It was a jasmine type tea that is sweet and light and fragrant. On the cover was a dragon.

"*Oh, how nice,*" the demoness said, "*but really, we don't need it. I have tea.*"

Father had warned me that demons sometimes do not have a feeling for the proprieties. It's always good on the first visit to bring a little something to drink or eat. If Father hadn't explained that to me carefully, I might have been offended by the demoness' refusal, because I might have mistaken her statement as saying that my gift was too cheap for her to use. I fumbled around for some excuse. *"Please. I drink lot. Too much. You take tea."* I thrust it out at her again. With a soft laugh, the demoness took it and lifted the lid. *"Why, there are flowers inside."*

She put water on to boil and then sat down across from me and picked at the tea until she could hold up one of the small white, delicate blossoms. *"Isn't that a lovely idea. Flowers in your tea."*

She got up and returned with a small white thingamabob that had thickened cow's milk in it. Thickened, yet! And it had an oily kind of smell that nearly made me sick. She also set down a sugar bowl. *"Cream and sugar, Moon Shadow?"*

"Oh, but you never put that into it!"

She stood with the sugar bowl in her hand. *"You don't?"*

"No. No. It ruin tea."

I will say this for the demoness. She was much more open to suggestion than I was. She put the sugar bowl and the—ugh—*cream* jar away, despite her misgivings. But after we had brewed the tea in the teapot, she sniffed at the spout appreciatively. *"Hmmm. But this does smell nice."*

And she poured out two cups of the amber liquid. She sipped it tentatively. I watched her face as she broke into her smile and drank more. At least I had broken her of putting cream and sugar into everything. We drank our tea in a friendly kind of silence, and then Miss Whitlaw picked up the box again. Her finger traced the long sinuous curves of the golden dragon. *"Oh, my, isn't it a"* —it sounded like—*"bu-dee-fu dragon?"*

"Please?"

"Beautiful," she repeated, and explained the word to me.

Once I understood her, I shook my head

vehemently. *"No, no. It a . . ."* I fumbled for the right word in the demon language, but all I could come up with was, *"a dragonee dragon."*

Another thing to say for the demoness was her genuine interest in learning about people as people. Where some idiot like myself would have been smug and patronizing, the demoness really wanted to learn. And like Father, she was not afraid to talk to me like an equal. *"I don't think I understand."*

"Dragon do terrible thing, yes," I said, struggling for the right words. *"But dragon, they do good thing too. Bring rain for crops. They king among all . . . all reptile. They emperor of all animal."*

And so on. I went on to tell the demoness everything my Father had told me about dragons.

"Why, how marvelous," the demoness exclaimed when I was finished. *"I never knew dragons did so much."*

"Maybe only bad kind go live here. You know, outlaw, that respectable dragon no want."

"Why, yes." The demoness nodded. *"That would make sense. All the dragons I've read about haven't been very pleasant creatures."*

"No dragon pleasant. A dragon dragonee."

At that moment, someone knocked on the door. I looked up at the clock on the demoness' cabinet. I had spent over an hour here. *"That my father,"* I said, frightened. *"He look for me."*

"It was my fault, so don't worry." She added something that sounded like *tee ah.*

"Please?"

The demoness looked embarrassed. *"I said 'dear'—it means a friend, or someone who is close to you."* She smoothed out a wrinkle in the tablecloth. *"Perhaps I was too forward."*

"No, no. It all right," I said. I felt sure now that I

had known the demoness, Miss Whitlaw, in some other life.

"*Why thank you,*" she said. The knock came again, more insistently this time. Miss Whitlaw opened the door.

"*Hello, Mr. Lee. Moon Shadow and I were just talking.*"

"*That boy, him talk too much,*" Father said sternly.

"*No, no, it was my fault, I'm afraid. I kept your boy here listening to the wanderings of an old lady.*"

"*You too kind,*" Father said.

"*On the contrary, you're too kind for loaning your son to me for all this time.*" Miss Whitlaw laughed pleasantly. "*When you get old, you get very selfish. Here I've kept Moon Shadow for so long and it's nearly three. I didn't even give a thought to getting dinner for my boarders either.*"

Miss Whitlaw had five *boarders* in her house. Each slept in his or her own room, but all of them ate at the dinner table with Miss Whitlaw. I only saw them once or twice, because the demons and demonesses were so old that they kept to themselves. Father and I excused ourselves then and left.

I had begun to think that the demons were not really so bad, but that very evening I found out that there can be some bad demons too. I was taking the trash out to the trash barrels when I saw a demon boy lounging against the wall of our alley. I was to find out later that he lived in the tenement house next door. He was about two or three years older than I was, and he was dressed in a gray shirt without a collar. The shirt was of a good, if rough, material. His hair was brown and his face was covered with brown spots—*freckles*, Robin told me later.

I passed by him, when he kicked me in the backs

of my legs. I fell on my back, cracking my head against the ground, the breath driven out of me. Our garbage pail spilled out all over the alley. The boy leered down at me. And above me, on the back landing of the tenement house next door, I saw a half dozen boys begin to shout.

> *Ching Chong Chinaman,*
> *Sitting in a tree,*
> *Wanted to pick a berry*
> *But sat on a bee.*

I jumped to my feet and made the mistake of trying to express my anger in the demon tongue. All I could come up with was, *"I no like you."*

The boys fell over one another laughing.

"You no likee me?" the boy asked mockingly. *"I no likee you."*

In my frustration, I began to curse him in the Tang people's language, using some of Uncle's more memorable curses. "I'm going to cut off your head," I told him, "and leave it in the gutter for the dogs to eat. . . ." I went on from there, embroidering on the scene, but the boy shinnied over the fence while the boys above him began to make mock Tang-people sounds—sounds like *"Wing-Duck-So-Long"* and *"Wun-Long-Hop"* in rising and falling voices. I could have bitten off my tongue. But I stood there, staring at them, not wanting to let them chase me away. I felt something soft and wet hit my leg. It was an old tomato. They began to throw bits and pieces of garbage at me. Still I stood there. Finally stones began falling around me. I suppose they had collected the garbage and the stones before they tried to get me. I felt a vague feeling of triumph at having made them use their biggest weapons.

I turned slowly, as if I were not afraid of them but only bored. A stone caught me in the small of the back. I grunted, but I took my time despite the pain, remembering how Red Rabbit had behaved that other time. Besides, I did not want to give them the satisfaction of seeing me cry.

I did not tell Father about the demon boys. He might have become worried and insisted that we go back to live among our own people—even if it meant swallowing his pride and settling up with the Sleepers.

The next day I tried to go with Father, but he said he was going into a rougher area that day, so I spent the whole time inside the stable. The demon boys must have played hooky that day. Every now and then I would hear them chant something, and sometimes rocks would thud against the walls. I did my best to go on with my chores and lessons, but it was hard.

It did not help my state of mind when Father came home that evening with a black eye and his right sleeve torn. He set down his tool box and pointed a finger at me. "Before you ask any questions, I'll just say that I got the best of a fight with two demons. They ambushed me inside one of Mr. Alger's buildings. I suppose they thought they could rob me."

I went out and got some water for Father to wash up. "Did they?" I asked.

Father grinned. "What do you think?"

During the next demon week, the nighttime was especially bad for me. I could imagine that every sound was made by demons or ghosts gathering in the dark to whisper by the door while they waited to pounce on me. It got so that I was afraid at night to go outside to the pump in the back yard, because I was afraid the demons might be attracted by the sound of splashing water. But I had to wash the dishes, so I would dash out to the pump. With my heart beating fast, I would prime the handle frantically and then run back to the shed as fast as I could, spilling half the water on the way.

It was the demon girl who started to wash her dishes outside for the "fresh air" instead of inside the kitchen at the indoor pump. Though I trusted Miss Whitlaw, I was not so sure about the demon girl. With her flaming red hair, she seemed like a true fox demoness who would delight in tricking humans.

Maybe she was just curious about why I rushed back and forth to the pump. But I still was not too sure about the demon girl, and I had heard about fox demonesses luring humans to their deaths. I stayed inside. Finally, the demon girl filled a bucket of water and pointed in my direction, meaning it was for me. I suppose she knew I was watching her from inside the stable.

But the next day, the demon girl was on the back porch peeling potatoes. And after that she peeled some apples. And after that she peeled some onions. She was laying siege to me. She stayed out there for most of the day, until I just had to make a trip to the outhouse. When I came out, I tried to walk quickly back to our stable, but she dashed down the steps and got in front of me. "Why are you scared of the pump?" she demanded. I shrugged silently. I trusted Miss Whitlaw not to make fun of my demon talk, but not anyone else.

"But it's stupid," the demon girl persisted. "You lose half the water your way." The demon girl pulled one of her pigtails over her shoulder in front of her so she could study its tip. "Are all Chinamen crazy like you?"

The kitchen door opened suddenly. "You, Robin,"

Miss Whitlaw said sternly. *"I told you to leave* Moon Shadow *alone."*

"But I'm just trying to be friendly with him, but he won't talk to me," protested Robin.

Miss Whitlaw leaned over and spoke gently. *"How would you feel if you were plunked right down in China in a small village with almost no hope of going back? Wouldn't you be scared?"*

"Well, yes," the demon girl admitted reluctantly. Then she looked at me. *"But I'd listen to some Chinaman who told me there wasn't anything in the village pump or anything near it that could hurt me."*

She walked back to the steps and picked up her bucket of potatoes and went inside. Miss Whitlaw stood helplessly by the door. *"I'm sorry,* Moon Shadow."

"It all right," I said. My cheeks were red with embarrassment.

That night I made myself join the demon girl by the pump to do the dishes. I had to prove to her I was not scared. But I still would not speak to her—and I wore the charm against demons. No sense in taking an extra risk.

It was about two demon weeks after the water-pump incident. The city had steady spring rains every day, but I didn't mind. The demon boys stayed inside, if they were around at all. Though Father was not at home, I had company enough, for the rains here were lively, friendly things. The strong winds would blow in from the sea and catch the rain, so that you never knew from what direction it would hit. Sometimes it would drum suddenly on the roof. The next moment the roof would be silent, as the rain rattled against the glass on one wall. Then the rain would jump and tap at the window on the opposite side.

During this time, Father lined up extra repair jobs—clocks and things to fix in his spare time until his table was cluttered. Still, he spared a half hour every evening to read to me from his *aeronautical* books. I don't think he ever stopped to consider that the *Wrights* were about the only demons to whom I could have talked for any long period of time. And after the half-hour lesson would come the reward, when we would work at a model of a glider, imitating the pictures and schematics in the books. Father would set the problem of ratios to me, in which I would have to convert the figures for a full-length original to a scaled-down model. Between my head and the abacus, I managed. Then Father and I would cut the bamboo strips and the rice paper and slowly construct the model. But we never got a chance to fly it, because whenever Father was free, it was raining.

So, came his first free day when the skies, though still cloudy, did not look like rain, Father announced we were flying it even though we had to wear boots and heavy coats. In those days *San Francisco* had not been built up as much, and if we walked about a mile to the west, we'd find plenty of open sand dunes for several miles until we hit the ocean. I might have known the demon girl would tag along.

She walked behind us, pretending to be interested in various houses and gardens that just happened to lie along the way we were taking. Finally after this had gone on for three blocks, Father turned. *"You want help us fly it?"* He held up the model glider. It was a good three feet in wingspan.

The demon girl shrugged. *"I guess so."*

I said nothing to her. I felt betrayed by Father, and I was hurt, too, that Father spent most of the time talking to the demon girl. He was only being polite, but I did not see it that way. I kept waiting for her to make fun of the way he talked, but she never did.

"*I've never seen a kite like that,*" she said finally.

"*This model of glider take man into sky,*" Father said.

"*Oh, go on.*" The demon girl shook her head. "*I wasn't born yesterday.*"

"*No, you born maybe ten years ago,*" Father said matter-of-factly, and was puzzled when the demon girl sniffed and her back stiffened—she was awfully touchy about people being smart with her, and she thought Father was being smart right then. He was only stating a fact, though, as he understood it. But the demon girl warmed up when we began to fly the glider. Father had me run with it while he jotted down notes with a well-worn stub of a pencil on some of our old bills. The glider behaved erratically, dipping and then soaring and then dipping again. Then Father waved me back to him. When I got there, we pulled in the glider. It came down too quickly, but Father ran and caught it.

Then he turned the glider model over in his hands. I took some more scraps of paper with clean backs out of his pocket. It was my turn to take notes (and also get some writing practice in demonic). "*It need more wing surface,*" Father mused. And he went into a lot of jargon about *center of gravity* and *wing configuration.*

"*Wing what?*" the demon girl asked.

Father glanced at me. It was my turn to show off. "*Wing configuration. You know, shape of wing.*" I traced the shape of the wing with my pencil. I waited for her to make fun of me.

"*Oh,*" was all the demon girl said. She crossed her arms. "*For someone who doesn't know English too well, you know an awful lot of four-bit words."*

"They in the books," I said cautiously.

"Books?" the demon girl asked. She picked up interest.

"We show," Father said politely.

When we returned to our stable, we gave the demon girl our one good chair—an old stool that Father had found in a vacated apartment and which we had stripped of paint and repainted. She sat down before our bookcase—several fruit crates turned on their sides. She paged through the books, looking more and more puzzled. *"You understand this?"* she asked.

"Yes, some," I said. Father nudged me and I stood beside her, explaining what I could in my broken demonic. In the meantime, Father left to buy some vegetables from a nearby greengrocer for our dinner.

The demon girl closed the book when I finished explaining the paragraphs, and she leaned forward, her body following the line of books. *"But where's the dragon book?"*

"What dragon book?"

"The one that you get all those stories about dragons from. Or did you just make up those things you told to my aunt?"

"I say true things."

"About dragons bringing rain to men? And about their being able to change their size and shape?" The demon girl looked skeptical.

"They true," I insisted.

The demon girl pursed her lips. *"In China?"*

"In whole world. You 'Mericans not know everything."

The demon girl considered that for a moment as she picked at the lint on her coat. *"I suppose,"* she said grudgingly. *"But then, you don't know everything either."*

That was true, but I did not much like admitting it. Instead I shrugged. *"But I know lots about dragons. You like dragons?"*

"I don't know. I never met one." She said that almost as a dare to me, but I did not back down. *"How you know? They can be tiny, tiny as flea. Maybe you hear voice speak to you from nowhere. That them as tiny, tiny as ant, only you no see. Or maybe take shape of men."*

The demon girl crossed her arms over her chest and leaned forward on her knees. *"Humph!"* She still looked doubtful. I couldn't understand her stubbornness in refusing to believe in dragons. I suppose for her part, she could not understand why I believed in them. She added, *"I'm from"*—it sounded like—*"Me-syu-ee."*

"Please?"

She spoke very slowly. *"Missouri. It's a state."*

"Is that like province?"

"I guess. What I mean is that I'm as stubborn as a Missouri mule."

"Please?"

"As my aunt says, it's a creature that pound for pound can out-ornery any other creature on God's earth."

"How you know true? I never see one."

"Sure, you have. There are lots of mules."

"But you know if any come from Missouri?"

"I guess so."

"How you know?" I asked triumphantly.

The demon girl made a small exasperated sound. She mulled that over for a while, chewing at her underlip. *"You're a clever, slippery creature, Moon Shadow,"* she grudged finally. *"I'll give you that much. You turned the tables around nice and neat."*

She glanced at me sideways and smiled again. *"And as for telling whoppers, there probably never was your like. You tell some mean stories about dragons."*

"Whoppers? Mean stories?"

"Oh, never mind." The demon girl slid the book back into the shelf. *"But I'd swear you have an imagination almost as good as E. Nesbit."*

"Who that?"

"A new writer." And she made me wait until she got some books from her room. They looked very interesting, but to my embarrassment I found that I had spent so much time learning *aeronautical* jargon, I had not picked up on the everyday talk. Still, I could look at the pictures while the demon girl outlined the story about flying carpets and phoenixes and magical amulets and cranky old sand elves who lived on beaches. She explained that a cousin of her father's lived now in *England* and shipped them here.

"I've got some of these, too," the demon girl pretended to say casually. She slipped some *dime novels* from behind her back. They were printed on cheap tan-colored paper with the most lurid paper covers, and they ranged across a wide variety of subjects. There were *Ned Buntline* specials about the adventures of *Buffalo Bill* in the wild, wild West (to me it was east, though, since I judged things geographically in relation to the Middle Kingdom). There were others about *Jesse James* and how he tortured his robbery victims. But her pride and joy were the *Nick Carter* detective stories, with a dead body on almost every page, as she boasted.

"Your cousin send these?"

She laughed. *"Oh, no. I got these from Maisie, next door. She's a girl in my class in school. She got them from her brother, Jack. We trade back and*

forth, but"—she leaned forward conspiratorially—
*"you can't tell Auntie. She'd have kittens if she found
out."*

"She would?" I said with interest.

*"No, no. It was only a figure of speech. I'd get in
trouble if she knew I was reading these,"* she said. I
realized then that the demon girl, Robin, was testing
me. Well, she was not all that bad to talk to, and she,
at least, had never thrown a rock at me.

"I no tell," I said.

She sat back, satisfied. *"You can read them if you
like."*

*"I like to, but I not think I can. Too many words
I not know,"* I confessed.

"I'll teach you," Robin said loftily. She put her
hand on the stack of E. *Nesbit* books. *"We'll start
with these and then when you know English better,
you can read these."* She touched her precious pile of
dime novels.

That was how my lessons started. Father gave me
permission to go over to Miss Whitlaw's for an hour
to read with Robin and write. Miss Whitlaw sat in
the parlor and helped me too. My vocabulary and
grammar picked up enough so that I could stumble
through the E. *Nesbit* books. I found that the *dime
novels* were easier stuff because they had simple
words and ideas. Robin was right. They were great.
"Awash with gore," she liked to say.

And even after I had finished the *Nesbit* books, we
continued my lessons. We would talk about any
number of things, and Miss Whitlaw encouraged me
to write short paragraphs about dragons, which she
and Robin then corrected. Robin, of course, said she
did not believe one word of what I wrote or said
about dragons. She would simply sniff or roll her
eyes or shake her head at another *whopper.* But she

was always there in the parlor, every night, munching away at cookies and listening to what I said or reading what I wrote about dragons, for I went on to tell them of the adventures of the dragons near my village—of their feuds and wars, of the love affairs between men and dragon maidens (who would take a human form), and of the friendships that had helped me.

In the weeks that followed, I found out that while I had set out to reeducate the demoness about dragons, she was educating me in the demonic language. After a while, we wandered away from dragons, for to explain about the dragons, I had to describe my home—I mean, our home.

In very halting demonic, I told them about the waters of the Pearl River: thick and milky and colored a reddish yellow like the color of sunset distilled from the air. On the river, you might see a stately junk, tottering its way upstream, slatted sails rising to meet the wind. And skittering all around them would be the small, two-man fishing boats like little water bugs skimming over the surface. Sometimes they sailed in pairs before the wind with a net between them, scooping up the fish. Their square sails danced before the wind like sheets of paper.

All this Miss Whitlaw listened to, and more. Oh, someone else might say that she was simply interested in a foreign country, but I was convinced that she hung on my words because she had been a Tang woman in a former and better life.

But if things were going great for me, I could not say the same for my father. There was so much to learn about the *aeroplanes*. There were tables and charts he needed for various things, like the ratio between the curvature of the *propeller* blades and the revolutions they produced. It was then that I got an idea. I waited until Robin was in school and Father was away on an errand before I went to see Miss Whitlaw.

"You help me write letter, maybe?" I asked her.

"Why, of course, Moon Shadow. *To whom are you writing?"*

"To the Wrights," I announced proudly. *"The aeronauts."*

Miss Whitlaw seemed impressed. *"Oh, yes. I've read all about their exploits, and if half of what they say is true, why it must be marvelous. But why do you ever want to write to them?"*

"My father," I began cautiously, *"he want fly like Wrights."*

Miss Whitlaw put a hand to her mouth. *"Oh, my. Isn't that rather dangerous?"*

I shrugged. *"Not if he know how."*

"Does he?"

"Yes and no," I said. I did not think Miss Whitlaw could be told about the dream. *"But he need facts, numbers, to build aeroplane."*

"Robin told me he made such marvelous glider models, but I had no idea it was only a preliminary. To have such ambition!" Miss Whitlaw shook her head in admiration—and I think also a little anxiously.

"You help me write to them?"

"Yes. Do you have their address?" When she saw my puzzled look, she explained the demons' postal system.

"I know village . . . no . . . the town they live in, and . . . and province . . . no, state."

"Well," she said, *"it might get through with just that."*

With her help, I finally wrote something like this:

To the honorable Wrights:
This is to inform you that I am a boy of eleven. I
have greatly admired your feats of daring. My father
wants to fly too. Can you help him? We need to know
how to shape the propellers. We need to know how
big the wings should be in order to lift my father into
the air. Father says that no one else in the whole
world knows as much as you do about aeroplanes.
Thank you.

And I signed it with the sounds of my name spelled
out in demon letters. I wrote several drafts of it and
then copied it out in the fine, elegant hand Miss
Whitlaw had taught me. The next day we went down
together and mailed the letter. *"You realize though,*
Moon Shadow, *that even if they were to get this*
letter, there is no guarantee that they'll answer it.
They're busy men, you know."

But two weeks later, I got a letter from the
Wrights' bicycle shop, and in a very neat, strong
hand *Orville* answered me:

Dear Mr. Lee,
My brother and I are always happy to meet
another flying enthusiast. Our brotherhood is too
small to lose any one of us. Enclosed you will find
some tables and diagrams that should prove of some
service to you. If we can be of any further assistance
to you, please let us know.

I waited anxiously that whole afternoon until
Father came home. I almost danced around him.

He hung his hat up on a nail and grinned. "What
is it you want to tell me? Did someone die and leave
us a fortune?"

"Better than that," I said. I held up the letter.

"I can't read that kind of demon script." Father handed the letter back to me. He could only read demon printed letters. He sat down on a crate while I read the letter to him. When I finished, I found him staring at me. I could not tell if he was angry or what.

"They also sent us some tables and diagrams. . . ." I tried to show them to Father but he would not look at them. "Did I do wrong?" I asked.

"It's just that . . . that it seems like begging," Father said.

"But Miss Whitlaw—"

"Miss Whitlaw?" Father asked sharply. "Did you ask her to write the letter?"

"She only helped." I set the tables and diagrams down on top of a nearby crate.

"You told her about my dream," Father accused me.

"No," I said quickly. I was scared.

"You talk too much," Father snapped. Father crumpled up the letter and threw it into a corner.

I left Father sitting in the stable. Miss Whitlaw and Robin were in the kitchen baking some things; but Miss Whitlaw took one look at my face and told Robin to leave the room. Then she sat me down at the table and took my hand.

"*What is it,* Moon Shadow?"

I told Miss Whitlaw about Father's being mad, and I hinted a little about how he behaved like a dragon sometimes. But Miss Whitlaw did not laugh.

"*Perhaps* . . ." Miss Whitlaw tapped a finger against her lips for a moment. "*Perhaps the truth of the dragon lies somewhere in between the American and the Chinese versions. He is neither all-bad nor all-good, neither all-destructive nor all-kind. He is a creature particularly in tune with Nature, and so, like Nature, he can be very, very kind or very, very terrible. If you love him, you will accept what he is. Otherwise he will destroy you.*"

For a long time, I listened in silence to the steady ticking of her kitchen clock. "*You wise woman,*" I said finally.

"No," she laughed. "*Just a foolish old woman who talks so much that every now and then she gets lucky and says the truth.*" She patted me on the shoulder. "*Now go back to him.*"

I went back. Rather than shout at me, Father had gone to sleep. The next morning, I found that Father had picked up the letter and smoothed it out on the table as best he could. At that moment, he was leafing through the tables and diagrams. He turned around when he heard me get up. "Still, there's so much to know. And they did call us brothers."

"Yes, they did," I said carefully.

Father shook the tin can into which we put our savings. He pulled out some demon paper *dollars* and coins. "Maybe they'd like a crate of oranges."

"Don't you want to write a letter to them?"

"Yes, I guess that would be best. Can you write while I dictate?"

"I can try."

Father thought for a moment. "Maybe you should get Miss Whitlaw to look at the final version," Father suggested. He wagged a finger at me. "But only for the grammar."

Chapter 8

Earth, Wind, and Water
(June–September, 1905)

That was how our correspondence began with the Wrights. *Orville* seemed to handle all their letter writing. He wrote impersonal letters, not because he was not a friendly man, but because he was the kind of man who did not often display his own inner emotions. He answered any of Father's questions readily enough, and his answers were always prompt. At that time few of their fellow demons believed that the Wrights had really flown. Most demons thought that the Wrights were humbugs. It was not until a few years later, when they flew their flying machine in another demon land—*France,* I think—that demons accepted flight as a fact.

After Father got the first letter, he began to make larger glider models. They were mock-ups of the actual aeroplane, with wingspans of up to five feet. There were extra strings that led to the various rudders. The idea was to let Father see for himself how the aeroplane flew. Short of going to the Wrights and letting them teach us on their actual flying machine, it was the only way of learning how to fly.

Robin was all excited by the mock-up gliders my father built. *"How does it fly?"* she demanded of the latest model.

"Like dream," I said. *"You ought see it ride winds. Like cloud."*

"Yes, we should see it," Robin said firmly. *"We'll have a picnic at the beach. We haven't had one in just ages."*

"What 'bout your aunt?" I asked.

"You leave my aunt to me," Robin said firmly. *"What about your father?"*

"You leave him to me," I said.

That Saturday we went on a picnic.

The morning of Saturday, Father glanced at himself in the mirror. "I can't go out like that." On impulse, he searched through our trunk and took out a long red silk ribbon.

"What's that?" I asked.

"Your mother gave me this ribbon," Father said almost shyly, "the first year we were married." He dangled the ribbon. "She said it was to be my formal suit of clothes."

He unbound his queue until his hair hung down loose on his back. Then he recombed it and rebraided the queue, intertwining the red ribbon through the braids. The red ribbon did make his hair look quite colorful, a little like the red lining around the scales of a black snake.

Miss Whitlaw came out fresh and pert as a young girl on her first date. She wore the large kind of broad-brimmed hat that women wore in those days, which she tied down with a scarf that she had knotted underneath her chin. She had on a kind of little jacket over her blouse. Under her arm was a straw hamper. *"I can't wait to see what you brought for our lunch,"* she said.

"Neither can I," Father said and explained that he had left all the buying up to me.

We caught the streetcar to the park and part of the way toward *Ocean Beach* in the west. We walked along the sand dunes that seemed to stretch endlessly away on either side. To the north, we could hear the barking of seals from where they basked on *Seal Rock.* Robin and I went wading in the water, splashing one another. Then we had lunch.

Miss Whitlaw had provided thick sandwiches with meat from a fat bird which the demons liked, a *turkey* I think it was called. Inside the sandwiches she had added slices of *cranberry sauce* as well as *bread stuffing.* I was barely able to get my mouth around one of them. There was also fresh lemonade, *gingersnaps,* and fresh fruit, and nuts which we cracked between rocks. At the same time I had brought along large meat-filled dumplings and other smaller pastries filled with various kinds of ground meat and shrimp. All of these I had bought in the Tang people's town that morning. There was tea, of course.

After that was over, Father lay on his back, patting his stomach. "I feel badly in need of some exercise," he said.

"Do you want to fly the glider?"

"I think it's time."

I turned to the others and told them.

"I-get-to-hold-the-string," Robin said in a rush of words.

"No," I protested. *"I do."*

"But I said it first." Robin turned to her aunt. *"Didn't I, Auntie?"*

"Now, Robin. It isn't ladylike to run," Miss Whitlaw cautioned.

"*But ladies first,*" Father said, "*then* Moon Shadow."

"*Oh, all right,*" I said sullenly. "*But I get hold it.*"

"*Go on, for all I care.*" Robin had already begun to unbutton her shoes. In those days, children wore heavy, practical shoes that felt like they would outlast a steel monument, so whenever you could go barefoot, you appreciated it. Robin picked up the roll of string while I picked up the glider.

"*Let's go over here,*" Robin said.

"*Why?*"

"*Because I want to.*"

I muttered something that she pretended to ignore. I followed her obediently over to where the sand dunes dropped sharply five or six feet to the beach itself. We had picnicked above the beach among the sand dunes, almost on a kind of plateau. She looked down the almost perpendicular slope. "*Ready?*" she asked over her shoulder.

"*Yes.*"

"*Here I goooooooo!*" Robin shouted as she plunged down the dune, her legs lost in a cloud of sand. Half-stumbling, she raced down the dry stretch of sand to the darker sand where the sea still rolled in and out. Her straw sailor hat flew off.

"*Robin,*" Miss Whitlaw shouted. But Robin was already a hundred feet away now, standing ankle-deep in the surf. The line was already taut.

"Let go," Father said. I did and the glider leaped out of my hands three feet into the air and hovered indecisively. Robin ran parallel to the surf line, her pigtails flying. The glider was one of Father's earlier models, without the rudder controls. It was really like a big box kite in some ways. Suddenly the sea winds caught the glider and lifted it upward toward the sun, veering and soaring like a thing alive, pulling stubbornly at the string. Robin had stopped way down on the beach, a solitary little figure with the waves washing her legs.

Father cupped his hands about his mouth. *"Give it more string,"* he shouted to her. *"Give it more string. It smells its home."*

And Robin did. She had to, or it would have been lost. Father went down then to fetch her hat. That long afternoon we took turns flying the glider. First Robin. Then me. Then even Miss Whitlaw.

"Flying is a rather exhilarating experience," she confessed to us. Her eyes were shining as a twist of her wrist sent the glider dipping and then rising.

By the end of the day it was Father's turn. I remember how he stood on the beach, his pants rolled up as he high-stepped, whooping and shouting, through the surf. Once he stumbled and went down in the water, but he came right back up, laughing and spluttering and spitting out seawater. Triumphantly he held up the string to show us he had held on to the glider.

The sunset was beautiful that day. The sun was a bright orange disc hovering over the sea, and the sunlight glittered on the surface like a web of light, or lace that ever changed its pattern. Clouds were coming in from the ocean now, and they were tinted a bright scarlet red as they bordered the sun; but the farther away they got, the more they showed a deep solemn purple, and beyond that . . . beyond that purple it was black. And in some patches you could see the stars, but I liked to think that they were not stars but the eyes of dragons watching us from above.

By now it was Robin's turn again with the glider. But first, before he had let her take it up, Father had brought out a long red strip of paper. Last night I had seen him copy out the poem from the strip Lefty had given him, but he would not tell me why. Father attached the poem to the glider like a tail. It was only then that he would let Robin take it up.

"Are the sunsets like this in China?" Miss Whitlaw asked.

"Yes, just as lovely. Must be lovely all round world."

We sat in silence at the thought of that, feeling suddenly peaceful and happy. But finally Miss Whitlaw looked at her father's old watch, which she had brought in the hamper. *"I do think it's time to be heading back."*

"Yes, I think so too," Father said quietly.

But he did not go for his boots or roll his trousers back down. Instead, he took the string from the astonished Robin. With one hand he held the string, and with the other he dipped into his pants pocket and pulled out his penknife. He put the string between his teeth and unfolded the blade. For one moment, he watched, satisfied, as the glider tugged at the string in his hand and the poem fluttered. Then, with a sudden sweep, he cut the cord.

"Mr. Lee," Miss Whitlaw said in horror.

"We make more," Father said. *"What I make one day, I do again."* And I knew he was thinking of more than just making glider models.

The glider shot upward, trailing the line behind it. It hovered for a moment like a sea bird waiting for the great sea winds to catch it up so it could range long distances—perhaps all the way to the Middle Kingdom. Then the winds took it and swept it upward toward the west, and it was gone.

Father calmly folded his knife. *"It better not hold on to it."* He added in the typical way of a Tang person, *"It bad glider anyway."*

Robin stared up at Father like he was crazy. "It

was a beautiful glider."

"You like one?" Father asked.

That won Robin over completely. *"You bet,"* she said.

"Robin," Miss Whitlaw snapped. *"Really, Mr. Lee. I don't know what's gotten into that greedy child."*

Father held up his hand. *"I take as compliment."* He turned to Robin. *"I make one for Moon Shadow, one for you, and one for your aunt,"* he said.

Robin looked up wistfully at the empty sky. *"But we have no glider now."*

"There be other days," I said.

And there were. And there were other things we did, too, like going for evening rides on the cable car to get away from the heat. We rode on the outside so the breezes would cool us off.

During this time, we were not completely cut off from the Tang people's town. Once a week, with my empty basket on my arm, I would walk the block down to the cable car line and ride a cable car over the steep hills into the Tang people's town. I could have walked that distance, but it was too risky when I was by myself. Once I was in the town, I would bring our letters and money to the headquarters of our district association so they could be sent home. Then I would pick up what letters had arrived and do some grocery shopping. By the time I caught the cable car back to Polk Street, my basket would be weighed down.

It was not until late July that we received a reply from Mother and Grandmother to the letter Father had written them in May. Grandmother's letter was full of anxious advice, but her chief warning was to boil any water before we drank it. The demons' water, she informed us, was not very safe. Mother offered more advice, and added that Father had been lucky that the man he had killed had had no close kinsmen, for that sort of thing had led to feuds in the past. Mother also said that she offered incense to the Listener as often as she could, asking the Listener to watch over us among the demons. Father was pretty sure they would be comforted by the letters we had written during the last two months, for they were full of our successes among the demons, and especially about our new friends.

But then came one Sunday in August. Father had to go to one of Mr. Alger's houses to fix some pipes that had just broken, so that left us without anything to do. But he had already made smaller glider models for the three of us.

"Why don't we go fly them?" Robin asked.

"I don't know," I said. I was reluctant to leave the house without Father because of the demon boys. I could hear them playing in the street outside.

"Oh, come on. I know an empty lot near here. It's real big and no trees, and it has some great winds."

"No, I rather stay here."

"Suit yourself," Robin said, *"'cause I'm going."*

I started to fix dinner to occupy myself. Robin came out with her glider under one arm. She stopped when she saw what I was doing. She always asked about everything I did when I made dinner. I think secretly she was hoping to catch me making a dish of dog's or cat's meat. But that day I was preparing squid.

"Ugh, what's that?" She made a face.

"Squid. Can't you tell?" I held up a bunch of tentacles about an inch long.

She took one and examined it with interest. *"Do you eat them like spaghetti?"* she asked.

I held up one three-inch tentacle. *"No, too small."*

She made a face. She was not afraid of frogs or snakes or the other things that demon girls were supposed to be afraid of. I approved of that. Coming from a farming family where everyone, including the women, worked beside the men in the fields, we were not afraid of mice or frogs. You might be more annoyed with them for the damage they did or the noise they made.

"Afraid?"

"Of course not," she snapped. *"You sure you don't want to go fly my glider with me?"*

"No."

Robin stood on the steps. She heard the shrill voices of the boys and suddenly she nodded her head as if she understood. I did not want to be patronized.

"Well, why don't you go fly your glider?" I demanded.

"Oh, I don't know," she said airily. *"It's a little too late to do it. I guess I should get dinner ready, too."* She kicked me lightly. *"Curse you for being a good influence on me."* She went back inside and came out a few minutes later with a pan of peas to be shelled. She had taken off her coat and had put away her glider. She watched as I finished cutting up the little squids and cleaning out the entrails that had become black with its ink.

"Oogh, that's disgusting," she said. She sat down beside me and put the pan on her lap. She set down a pot next to her. *"I'm not scared, mind you, just disgusted."*

"Sure," I said.

She broke the pods with crisp snapping sounds. *"But I will own up to being scared of thunder."*

"Lot of people scared."

She went on breaking pea pods into the pot. *"But*

now you take that Jack," she said. *"You know him. He's the boy with the brown hair and the freckles. Well, he's the biggest boy in our school, and yet I happen to know personally from Maisie, his sister, that he'd rather die than let anyone know he was afraid of being hit in the nose, 'cause he's scared of the sight of blood—especially his."*

She studied me for a moment. She and I both knew the dragonish thing to do. Then she went back to shelling the peas. Outside in front of the house I could hear the voices of *Jack* and his gang. I began to shell peas for a while. Robin and I both knew I did not walk on Polk Street much because of the demon boys. Suddenly I put the last peas into the pot and got up.

Robin raised her eyebrows. *"Going for a walk?"*

"A little one," I said.

Jack immediately stopped playing mumblety-peg when he saw me. He took his penknife and drove it point first into the dirt of the alley. He got up with a big grin, and he and his friends gathered by the alley.

"Ching Chong—" he began.

"I no like that song," I said.

"Too bad," Jack said.

"I think it stupid."

"You saying I'm stupid?"

"Everyone know that."

Jack charged me with a shout. His friends behind him began to yell with shrill, excited voices. I am not much of a fighter and I never will be. There was as much luck with me that day as anything else. I was smaller and maybe quicker, but with his long arms and his strength, Jack could have strung me from a lamppost. But Grandfather and the other Old Ones must have been there to help me at that moment. Jack expected me to run, probably; he never expected me to stand up and fight, and he did not even think of dodging. I swung out and my fist went right into his face. Jack sat down with a plop in the dirt, blood running down from his nose.

"You hit me," he said in surprise.

"What you expect?" I asked. I doubted if I would ever get such a lucky punch in again. Still, I had come out here for the satisfaction of giving one punch to Jack for all the times he had tormented me—even if it meant getting beaten up in the end. I put up my fists awkwardly, ready to fight him some more. But Jack did not get up. The other boys behind him had grown silent.

"It's bleeding too," Jack said, holding up a hand to his face. *"And my mom just cleaned this shirt. She'll kill me."*

"Tough." I just wanted to get the rest of the beating over with by that time. I held my fists ready to hit him.

"Jesus, but you're a scrappy little son of a"—it sounded like—*"bit-sha, aren't you?"* Jack muttered.

"Bit-sha?" I said the word I didn't recognize.

"Shhh," Jack said. *"Not so loud, or we'll get our mouths washed out with laundry soap."*

He held out his bloody hand. I took it and helped pull him up. Suddenly I realized that these demons were like the Tang boys I knew at home. You only had to punch out the biggest and toughest of the bunch and the others would accept you. Well, Jack was the biggest and toughest of his group. He looked down at me. *"Say, you know, you're all right, Chinaboy,"* he said.

"I not Chinaboy," I said.

"Whatever you say," he said. And I knew I would not have to worry about wearing Hand Clap's charm after that. I don't mean to sound like all my problems

with the demons were solved, or that I stopped wearing the charm completely. There was only one particular group of demon boys I did not have to watch out for; I still had to be careful whenever I left the stable. It's just that I was sure now that I could handle anything I met: My fists and my brains and my feet were as good a set of charms as the charm from Hand Clap.

Sometimes the month of September in the demon city could be just as hot as August. And it was on one such evening that we went out into the back yard because the house and stable had not cooled off as fast as the outside. We sat in chairs that we brought out.

Robin, who knew something of the stars, began to name the constellations for us. *"See that milky streak there? That's the Milky Way. And on one side you see Aquila. That's Latin for eagle. And on the other side you see Lyra, the Lyre—that's a kind of harp."*

"That constellation you call Eagle. What you call that star?" Father pointed to the brightest star.

"Altair."

"And bright star of Lyre?"

"Vega."

"Well, if you take those three stars of your Eagle and forget 'bout others, you get what we call the Cowherd. And if you take those three stars of Lyre and forget about other stars, you get . . ." Father turned to me. *"What you call it?"*

"Spinning Maid," I said.

"Just so," Father said. And he went on to tell their story. How long ago, an angel who kept the herd of cows in the sky married an earth girl, the Spinning Maid, and took her to live with him in Heaven. They spent so much time together that they did not do their

work. The cows wandered all over Heaven and cloth did not get woven. The untended cows trampled into the palaces of the gods, and the gods themselves began to wear tattered robes because there was no cloth from which to make new ones. Finally, the Jade Emperor decided that the situation was impossible. "We must separate the two," he said.

And his wife, taking a hairpin from her hair, dug a great ditch across the sky and created a river filled with a silvery white liquid, which Robin called the *Milky Way* but which we called the Silver River. The two lovers wept so much that the Jade Emperor took pity on them and told them that on the seventh day of the seventh month, they could visit one another. And on that night, all the magpies of the world gather together at the river and form a bridge, their wings interlaced, and they stay there even though the passing lovers wear the feathers off their heads and wings.

"But that's such a sad story," Robin said.

"Yes, it is," Father said. But I saw he was looking up at the Silver River and thinking not of the story but of Mother and himself. Only between them, no magpies formed a bridge across the oceans. Miss Whitlaw realized that too, I think, and so she changed the subject.

"So tell me, Mr. Lee—if we took our constellations and broke them up into bits, and then reassembled them using the pieces of the different constellations, we would get the Chinese constellations?"

"Yes," Father said.

"We see the same thing and yet find different truths," Miss Whitlaw mused. She pointed up at another group of stars. *"What do you call that, Robin?"*

"The Twins," she said.

I turned to Father. *"And what you call that?"*

And Father perked up as he showed the Whitlaws how to realign them into another shape and told the story of that. Miss Whitlaw encouraged Father for a bit longer, until he and Robin began naming constellations and then rearranged the stars into other shapes. I looked at Miss Whitlaw. She winked at me. She had distracted Father.

Chapter 9

The Dragon Wakes
(December, 1905–
April, 1906)

By the time the winter rains came to the city, we were not becoming rich, but we were doing well. Each day we put a little money away in our old tin can. Father never said anything, but I knew he was thinking about the day when we might be able to afford to bring Mother over. You see, it was not simply a matter of paying her passage over on the boat. Father would probably have to go over after her and escort her across. There had to be money for bribes—tea money, Uncle called it—at both ends of the ocean. Now that we no longer belonged to the Company, we somehow had to acquire a thousand dollars worth of property, a faraway figure when you can only save *nickels* and *dimes*.

And yet the hope that we could start our own little fix-it shop and qualify as merchants steadily grew with the collection of coins in the tin can. I was happy most of the time, even when it became the time for the New Year by the Tang people's reckoning—our New Year came a few months after the demons' New Year and our celebrating lasted for several days. Traditionally, it was a time for paying your debts and patching up any quarrels that may have occurred during the year. I had hoped that Uncle and Father would make up so we could spend Father's day off or at least an evening celebrating the New Year with the Company, but both Father and Uncle kept quiet. They were still hurt with one another; and perhaps, too, they did not trust their tempers yet. The first week of the New Year is no time to become angry. Instead, we stayed at home in the stable, but we were not alone. Robin came to help us with the New Year's feast.

We took the old picture of the Stove King and smeared some honey on it before we burned it in the stove. Later that evening we would hang up a new picture of the Stove King that we had bought in the Tang people's town. That was a sign the Stove King had returned to his place above our stove. After we had finished burning the old picture, we sat down to a lunch of meat pastries and dumplings. Robin ate quietly—for her, that is. Actually, she monopolized only half the conversation. *"Look,"* she said. *"My aunt would never go in for those pagan customs— not in her house. But I could sneak the old picture out and tell her you wanted to replace it with a new one. Then you could smear honey on it for her."*

"But you no believe in the Stove King."

"Of course not," she snapped. She squirmed in her seat. *"But it might make you feel better."*

I could see that she really wanted to make herself feel better. No sense taking chances with the supernatural, and so on. I could tell her train of thought because I sometimes carried the little cross she had given me in my pocket—just as insurance. I mean, maybe *American* demons could be scared off by *American* charms.

"*Sure, why not?*" I said, feeling a little triumphant. I set to the dumpling on my plate while the rain fell steadily on the roof. Later Robin took her umbrella and fetched back the Stove King. We smeared extra honey on it— Father was not going to take chances. And then we burned it too. When it came time to hang up our new picture, I took out the extra picture of the Stove King that I had bought just in case Robin did decide to celebrate the New Year properly. With a satisfied smile, I gave it to her.

And then as the winter rains gave way to spring, Uncle took the first step toward making peace. It was near the time of the Feast of Pure Brightness, when we go out to the graves and make offerings to the dead. It's not nearly as somber as it sounds. It is really the major festival for the springtime. We go out to the graves and sweep them and clean them and tell the dead about some of the things that have happened. Then we make them offerings of food, only we don't give all of it to them. After all, it's a banquet where we all share. So we take home some of the better things to eat, knowing the hungry dead will be happy. Unlike the other holidays, it is determined by a solar calendar like that of the demons, and so it is always on April 5.

The Tang people's cemetery at that time was not a permanent one. All Tang people wanted to be buried finally in their homeland. But there were often delays of several years between when a man died and when his body got shipped home. So there was a cemetery where the coffins were temporarily buried.

Old Deerfoot, a houseboy in a mansion a few blocks away from us, came over one day. He did not rush into his business the way a demon might have.

We spent a half hour over tea, talking about the Tang people's town and our respective families back in the Middle Kingdom, and how the boycott had affected them. The Tang people at home had tried to boycott demon goods until the demons stopped persecuting the Tang people over here in the Land of the Golden Mountain, but it had failed. It was not until the second cup of tea that Old Deerfoot got around to the purpose of his visit.

"The Feast of Pure Brightness is only a few weeks away," he said with a sigh. "Where does the time go?"

"It goes too fast," Father agreed.

Old Deerfoot shook his head. "I've way too many friends out there, biding their time till they go back home."

"I don't have nearly as many as you do, but I have a few too." Father held the cup between his two hands.

"Then you'll be going out?"

"I don't know yet. The demons keep me pretty busy."

"Well, if you'll be needing a lift out there," Deerfoot said with pretended casualness, "your uncle said he would be going."

"He did, did he?" Father finished the rest of his tea and pursed his lips while he thought. He looked at me. "What do you think?"

"It isn't my place to think," I said.

Deerfoot laughed and Father made an exasperated sound. "You know very well you'd like to go out with them." I just stood silent. Father turned to Deerfoot. "Tell Uncle we'd . . . we'd appreciate the lift."

"Good," Deerfoot smiled. We drank two more cups of tea before it was a proper time for him to leave. As I washed the dishes, I said nothing. I did not even smile. But inside, I secretly thanked the Stove King perched above our stove.

Early that morning, they pulled up in front of the house. We stood up from where we had been sitting on the front steps. I looked up at Father. He felt as shy as I did. Hand Clap was riding on the front seat of the wagon, the reins held loosely in his hands. He nodded to us.

Father nodded back and slapped Red Rabbit on the rump. "Is he giving you any trouble?"

"No," Hand Clap said. "He's still the laziest horse in the demon land."

Father stuffed his hands back into his pockets. "He's really not all that bad."

"Oh, no?" Hand Clap raised his eyebrows. "We started out yesterday morning just to get here."

"Hah," Father said. He reached over the side of the wagon and held out his hand, demon style, to the others. "You're getting fatter, Lefty."

"Me? You're the one who's bursting his clothes at the seams."

Father shook White Deer's hand. "You haven't started to sprout flowers yet. That's good."

"You. You haven't had enough vegetables. I see the red choler in you," White Deer laughed.

Finally Father took Uncle's hand. "How are you, old man? Thought we'd be burying you this year instead of visiting the cemetery with you."

Uncle snorted. "Well, you young ones try, but if fifty years of demons couldn't put me under, you young punks aren't likely to." He leaned on the side of the wagon, looking down at Father with gruff good humor. "You are looking good and prosperous."

"Well enough. These demons don't seem to understand their own machines."

Then Uncle looked at me. He waved his hand. "Come closer, boy. I'm not going to bite off your ear." I stepped closer.

"How are you, Uncle?"

"Very well, for all you cared, you young scamp." He playfully boxed my ears. "You turn twelve and you forget all about us. How come you never came by?"

Father put his hands on my shoulders. "I'll have a talk with this boy, Uncle. He'll be by more often—even if I have to drag him into the store."

"You do that." Uncle smiled and his whole face wrinkled upward in those happy curves. "Now get on the wagon before that overfed, underworked horse of ours dies of old age."

You would think after that, that I would be happy. But I began to get uneasy.

Thinking of the dead, I began to think about how quickly things pass by in this world. I had a feeling that all of this was likely to disappear, as if I was like one of the heroes, in the old tales, who comes upon a golden palace and is welcomed inside by the palace folk and they are all beautiful and handsome and richly clothed. They wine him and dine him and sing to him until they put him to bed. The man goes to sleep in a golden palace and wakes up in a set of ruins, for the man had been the victim of illusions conjured by the demons. I had the feeling at times that our home, Miss Whitlaw, and Robin would all be gone the next morning when I woke up. I was not far from wrong.

It was thirteen days after the Feast of Pure Brightness that the earthquake hit. Just a little after five A.M., demon time, I had gotten dressed and gone out to the pump to get some water. The morning was filled with that soft, gentle twilight of spring, when everything is filled with soft, dreamy colors and shapes; so when the earthquake hit, I did not believe it at first. It seemed like a nightmare where everything you take to be the rock-hard, solid basis for reality becomes unreal.

Wood and stone and brick and the very earth became fluidlike. The pail beneath the pump jumped and rattled like a spider dancing on a hot stove. The ground deliberately seemed to slide right out from under me. I landed on my back hard enough to drive the wind from my lungs. The whole world had become unglued. Our stable and Miss Whitlaw's house and the tenements to either side heaved and bobbed up and down, riding the ground like ships on a heavy sea. Down the alley mouth, I could see the cobblestone street undulate and twist like a red-backed snake.

From inside our stable, I could hear the cups and plates begin to rattle on their shelves, and the equipment on Father's work table clattered and rumbled ominously.

Suddenly the door banged open and Father stumbled out with his clothes all in a bundle. "It's an earthquake, I think," he shouted. He had washed his hair the night before and had not had time to twist it into a queue, so it hung down his back long and black.

He looked around in the back yard. It was such a wide, open space that we were fairly safe there. Certainly more safe than in the frame doorway of our stable. He got into his pants and shirt and then his socks and boots.

"Do you think one of the mean dragons is doing all this?" I asked him.

"Maybe. Maybe not." Father had sat down to

stuff his feet into his boots. "Time to wonder about that later. Now you wait here."

He started to get to his feet when the second tremor shook and he fell forward flat on his face. I heard the city bells ringing. They were rung by no human hand— the earthquake had just shaken them in their steeples. The second tremor was worse than the first. From all over came an immense wall of noise: of metal tearing, of bricks crashing, of wood breaking free from wood nails, and all. Everywhere, what man had built came undone. I was looking at a tenement house to our right and it just seemed to shudder and then collapse. One moment there were solid wooden walls and the next moment it had fallen with the cracking of wood and the tinkling of glass and the screams of people inside.

Mercifully, for a moment, it was lost to view in the cloud of dust that rose up. The debris surged against Miss Whitlaw's fence and toppled it over with a creak and a groan and a crash. I saw an arm sticking up from the mound of rubble and the hand was twisted at an impossible angle from the wrist. Coughing, Father pulled at my arm. "Stay here now," he ordered and started for Miss Whitlaw's.

I turned. Her house was still standing, but the tenement house to the left had partially collapsed; the wall on our side and part of the front and back had just fallen down, revealing the apartments within: the laundry hanging from lines, the old brass beds, and a few lucky if astonished people just looking out dazedly on what had once been walls. I could see Jack sitting up in bed with his two brothers. His mother and father were standing by the bed holding on to Maisie. Their whole family crowded into a tiny two-room apartment. Then they were gone, disappearing in a cloud of dust and debris as the walls and floor collapsed. Father held me as I cried.

Miss Whitlaw came out onto her porch in her nightdress and a shawl. She pulled the shawl tighter about her shoulders. *"Are you all right?"*

"Yes," Father said, patting me on the back. "Aren't we, Moon Shadow?"

"Yes." I wiped my eyes on my sleeves.

"Is everyone okay inside?" Father asked Miss Whitlaw.

She nodded. We joined her on the porch and walked with her into her house. Robin was sitting on the stairs that led up to the second floor. She huddled up, looking no longer like the noisy, boisterous girl I knew. The front door was open before her. She must have gone outside to look. *"Just about the whole street's gone."*

From up the stairs we could hear the querulous old voices of the *boarders* demanding to know what had happened. Miss Whitlaw shouted up the stairs, *"Everything's all right."*

"Are you sure?" Father asked quietly.

Miss Whitlaw laughed. *"From top to bottom. Papa always built well. He said he wanted a house that could hold a herd of thundering elephants—that was what he always called Mama's folks. He never liked them much."*

"It's gone," Robin repeated. *"Just about the whole street's gone."*

"Oh, really now." Miss Whitlaw walked past Robin. We followed her out the front door to the front porch. Robin was right. No one had constructed the houses along the street as well as Miss Whitlaw's father had built his.

A strange, eerie silence hung over the city. The bells had stilled in their steeples, and houses had stopped collapsing momentarily. It was as if the city itself were holding its breath. Then we could hear the hissing of gas from the broken pipes, like dozens of angry snakes, and people, trapped inside the mounds, began calling. Their voices sounded faint and ghostly, as if dozens of ghosts floated over the rubble, crying in little, distant voices for help. Robin and I pressed close to one another for comfort. It was Miss Whitlaw who saved us. It was she who gave us something important to do and brought us out of shock.

She pressed her lips together for a moment, as if she were deciding something. *"We must get those people out."*

"It would take four of us weeks to clear tunnels for them," Father said.

"We'll draft help. After all, we were put on this earth to help one another," Miss Whitlaw said.

Father suppressed a grin. *"I see what can do. But better put on clothes."*

"What? Oh, my." Miss Whitlaw was suddenly horrified to be found in her nightgown in public. *"Come, Robin."* She took her by the hand and practically pulled her up the steps.

Father shook his head affectionately. He sat down on a chest in the hall and he and I began braiding up his queue. On his advice, we both pinned our queues into tight buns at the back of our heads. When we got outside the house, though, Father stopped. "I've put my boots on the wrong feet." Sure enough, he had his left boot on his right foot and vice versa. We both laughed a little louder than the joke actually deserved, but we were just so relieved that we were still alive after the disaster. Father sat down on the sidewalk and got his boots on right. He stood up, stamping his feet back into his boots. Then we looked around.

We had gone to sleep on a street crowded with buildings, some three or four stories high and crowded with people; and now many of the houses were gone, and the ones that remained were dangerously close to falling too. There was a hole in the cobblestone street about a yard wide and twenty feet long. As we watched, a cobblestone fell over the edge, clattering ten feet to the bottom.

I heard one person compare it to being on the moon. It was that kind of desolate feeling—just looking at huge hills of rubble: of brick and broken wooden slats that had once been houses. On top of the piles we would see the random collection of things that had survived the quake: somebody's rag doll, an old bottle, a fiddle, the back of an upholstered chair . . . and a woman's slender wrist, sticking out of the rubble as if calling for help.

And then the survivors started to emerge, and I saw that there were as many hurt in mind as in body. Some people wandered out of the buildings almost naked, others still in their nightclothes. I saw one man with the lather on one side of his face, the other side already clean-shaven. In his hand was a lather-covered razor. One woman in a nightgown walked by, carrying her crying baby by its legs as if it were a dead chicken. Father caught her by the shoulder and gently took the baby from her.

"Fix her arms," Father told me. I set her arms so she could cradle the baby—as if the mother were a doll. Then Father put the baby back into her arms. She dumbly nodded her thanks and wandered on.

Other people who had taken the time to dress had dressed in the oddest things, choosing things they wanted to save rather than what would be appropriate for a disaster. I saw one shopgirl go by in a ball gown with the ruffles sounding crisp in the morning air. Perhaps she had saved for a year to buy it. I don't know. But I saw another man in formal tails go by. His wife carried the baby while he pushed a baby carriage filled with jewelry, a frying pan, and a candelabrum.

Then along came a big healthy man with ginger whiskers. He had slipped his trousers on over his red *long johns.* In his arms he had a chest.

Father tried to stop him. *"Please—need help."* Father pointed to the mound behind us, from which the ghostly voices were calling.

"Be off with you," said the man.

Father tried grabbing him by his blue suspenders, but the man dodged away and started running. We tried to get other survivors to help. One or two came out of their daze and started to work on the mound, clearing rocks and broken boards again, but most of them ignored Father and went on their way as if they were made of stone. Some even cursed him.

Then Miss Whitlaw and Robin joined us. Both of them were in clean dresses, with their hair braided and coiled around their ears. You would have thought they were going to church. *"Please help us save the others,"* Miss Whitlaw said to two sturdy young men, but they were in a hurry pushing their wheelbarrow.

"Out of the way, you old bat."

"Well," sniffed Miss Whitlaw as they trundled past. *"You . . . you Sunday Christians,"* she called after them, as if it were the worst thing she could think of. She stood for a moment in the street, fingering the ends of her shawl. Then she turned around with a determined set to her jaw. *"Mr. Lee, I think we are going to have to use a more forceful argument than moral persuasion."* With that, she

marched back into her house.

Father scratched his head. *"What kind that?"* he asked Robin.

She shrugged. *"Maybe we'll pay them."*

Miss Whitlaw came out a moment later with one of her heavy wooden kitchen chairs. She set it down in front of Father. *"Please break this, Mr. Lee."*

Father shrugged and grasped the chair. He lifted it up high over his head and brought it down with a loud, splintering crash. Miss Whitlaw sifted through the broken wood. She handed one chair leg to Robin, one to me, and one to Father. She waved her own chair leg like a club. *"There never was anything like a swat across the fundament to wake up a sluggish conscience."* She pointed her club across the street. *"You take that side, Mr. Lee. I'll take this. Don't let anyone through."*

"What about your boarders?"

"Those ancient rabbits are packing their bags and running away." Miss Whitlaw sniffed. *"They're too old to help."*

It was a wonder to watch Miss Whitlaw sail up the block and gather people behind her like a hen collecting her chicks. In her gentlest but firmest way, she gathered up the surviving demons and set them in work crews to clearing the mounds from which people were calling.

Watching her with open admiration, Father shook his head. "Now just look at her." For myself, I could not help thinking that she had missed her vocation as a shanghaier.

The next moment I learned why we had clubs. A demon came toward us in a suit and balancing three hats on his head; two were derbies and the last was a top hat. In either hand he had a suitcase. His eyes glanced up continually toward his hats.

"Please help," Father asked him.

"Go on with you," the man said, and tried to push past.

Father shoved the end of his club into the demon's chest. *"You help."*

The demon dropped his suitcases and swung at Father, but Father ducked easily. He clubbed the demon lightly on the back of his head. The demon grunted and fell to his knees. Father raised his club menacingly.

The demon held up his hand. *"All right. All right. Just don't hurt the hats. Watch where you're stepping."*

"You go over there." Father pointed to where Miss Whitlaw stood supervising one reluctant work crew. The demon picked up his suitcases while Father picked up his hats, dusted them off, and set them on his head one by one.

I don't think the demons were necessarily bad for not wanting to help others. They might have been scared, or so shocked they could not really know how selfish they were being. Now that there were other demons actually helping to save the trapped demons, we did not seem to have as much trouble as before. Some demons were glad to pitch in. Though we still had to use the clubs on some others. When we had work crews at every mound from which there was a voice—about fifty people in all—we tucked our clubs into our belts and joined them. Miss Whitlaw had managed to salvage shovels, pickaxes, and crowbars from the various places for at least a dozen workers. The rest of us used our hands or the ends of boards.

Father deliberately chose to work on one mound which stood under a wooden wall. It was the last wall of the tenement—one of the buildings he had worked in—and at any moment the wall threatened to collapse. When I climbed up the hill of rubble to stand beside him, he turned to me. "You work somewhere else," he told me.

But I figured I had as much right to make a fool of myself as he did. I picked up a rock and sent it clattering down the slope of the hill-like mound.

Father tapped me on the shoulder. "Did you hear me, boy? You go someplace else."

"The faster we can clear this stuff away, the sooner we can leave this mound. Maybe we can even get away before the wall collapses."

Father grinned suddenly. "You're getting as unruly as a demon." He slapped me on the back, and together we went back to work.

As we worked to clear the mound, we saw five old demons and demonesses hobble down the steps of Miss Whitlaw's house. There were suitcases in their hands and some had to use canes to walk. They all had the same panicky look on their faces. It was the first time I had ever really seen them, and Robin was right when she told me they were enough to curdle milk. I felt sorry for her having to sit at the table with those old bags.

I went back to help clearing the mound. It was a little bit like playing *jackstraws,* where you toss all the straws down in a pile and then try to take one away without disturbing the others. There was a kind of science to freeing the demons from the mound. A building does not collapse completely. There are little pockets inside the mound where the people are trapped. The trick is to not dig away the whole mound, but to work tunnels to those pockets. But you have to be careful not to make the mound collapse on that pocket or on you. We picked up bricks, the rocklike broken bits of concrete blocks, the wooden boards. And Miss Whitlaw was everywhere, encouraging here, helping there. I wondered again at the strength within her slender body.

About an hour after we started, Miss Whitlaw came over with Robin in tow. All our sweating faces were covered with a fine film of dust. We all looked like the mountain trolls who live deep, deep within the earth. "Moon Shadow, *you and Robin make some sandwiches and hot tea. We'll all be needing a break.*"

I glanced up at the tottering wall. "It's all right," Father told me. "We're almost finished here." We had already pulled four people from the mound. Only one of them had any injury, and that was a broken leg.

Robin and I went around to the back. We were going to try to wash our hands and faces at the outdoor pump, but no matter how much we primed the handle no water would come out, so we decided to use the one in Robin's kitchen. But the indoor pump was dry too. There was only the steady crea-creak-creak as we took turns working the handle.

"*That's funny,*" she said. "*It's never been this slow before.*"

"*What do we use for water?*" I asked.

"*Get the water from the pitchers in the rooms,*" Robin said. There was a pitcher of water and a washbasin in each bedroom for washing up. She wagged a finger at me. "*And don't let me catch you wasting any of it by washing your face.*"

"*I wouldn't think of it,*" I said, though I really had been.

It was a good thing that Miss Whitlaw had just baked the other day, so there was plenty of white, fresh, sweet-tasting bread. For filler we had ham and some of that fermented cow's milk that the demons call cheese but that I always thought of as stuff made out of a cow's pale urine. It sure smelled like old urine to me. Luckily, there were also a lot of jellied preserves. Robin carried the sandwiches out on trays. I lugged the pail of water with the pitcher.

As the people quit working to gather round, Robin warned them that it was all the water we had until the pump started working, so they were to go easy.

Father paused, his sandwich in his hand.

"What's the matter?" I asked him. He seemed troubled. "Nothing," he said and went back to eating.

After breakfast, we went back to work. By that time, we had saved about twenty people. Poor Maisie and Jack had not been among them. Their bodies were still somewhere in the ruins of their tenement. We had put the three injured demons on makeshift stretchers, made out of blankets and long boards we salvaged from the ruins, and taken them into Miss Whitlaw's house, which was the only one standing intact on the block. Then she had sent one of the neighborhood boys—one of my former tormentors after a doctor.

We had not been at work again for more than a half hour when we heard an indignant yell that carried along the street. It was Robin. *"Hey, you, drop that."* Father and I turned to see a demon standing on the porch of Miss Whitlaw's house. He cradled a small metal chest in his arms. Father and I were working on a mound next to the house. Father jumped over Miss Whitlaw's fence. I was still climbing over it as Father ran across the garden to the bottom step. The thief stared at Father for a moment.

Then the demon tried to kick Father, but Father caught his leg and gave it a vicious twist. The thief had to turn around or lose his leg. Father shoved and the thief went face down on the porch. He rolled over, his hands reaching for his belt, but Father already had one knee on his throat. The thief lay still. Father slipped the knife out of his belt and threw it into the doorway. He handed the chest of money back to Miss Whitlaw.

She took it with a nod of thanks.

"Let him go now, Mr. Lee."

"But—"

"This earthquake'll bring out the best and worst in folk." Miss Whitlaw waved her hand as if the thief were some stray dog. *"Go on."*

The thief got up, not quite believing that he was free. Rubbing his throat, he limped down the steps and down the street with everyone staring.

"Better take inside and hide," Father said. Miss Whitlaw nodded and left. We heard her quick, light steps on the stairs. We both watched the thief slip around the corner, out of sight. "People," Father said with a shake of his head. "And this is probably only the start."

"Father?"

'There's a whole city in ruins, and more of his kind willing to take advantage of others' misery," he explained. He touched the club in his belt. "But there's no helping other people's souls. We can only try to help the people trapped inside the rubble."

About an hour later, we stopped. My throat was dry from the dust and dirt. I went to the outdoor pump and worked at it hard for about five minutes but still no water. And then, turning, I saw an ominous sight. There were three tall columns of black smoke rising from the south. They were apart from one another, but as I watched two more sprang up. I went quietly to Father and pulled at his sleeve.

He turned, heaved a stone down. He looked in the direction I pointed. "Yes," he grunted. "I noticed them. There's not enough pressure in the pipes for the water to come out of the firedemons' hoses."

"They'll fix them soon."

"Not soon enough if there's fires. There won't be any water for the firedemons to use." He put his hand on my shoulder. "But don't you tell anyone. No sense causing a panic. They might get the pipes fixed before there's a serious fire."

And he went back to work.

But it was not more than five minutes later that a buggy dashed by. There were a demon and a demoness and two frightened demon children clinging to it. To the top of the buggy were lashed a mattress, a nightstand, and other items. Pots and pans had been tied to the sides, and they clanked and rang as the man drove.

He had to stop when he came to the hole in the street. His horse was covered with sweat, as if the demon had driven him too hard. The demoness took the reins while he got down and threw his coat over the horse's eyes. He was wearing a bright pink nightshirt underneath. He guided the horse around the hole. Father went down to him then. "*What hurry?*" he asked.

"*There's a fire south of Market,*" the demon said. *Market Street* was the main street of the city and ran diagonally across it, dividing the city in half. "*There's no water for the hoses. They're still going to try to make a stand on Market, but I don't see what they can do. The fire'll just spread and spread.*"

Others had stopped work to look at the man. They began to throw down their tools and leave the rubble mounds. Miss Whitlaw stepped to the center of the street and held out her arms. "*We still have time,*" she pleaded. *"Please help."*

But they all ignored her. The demon got back into his buggy and slapped the horse's rump with the reins. The buggy clattered on over the cobblestones. When I looked back, the entire street was abandoned, except for a few people trying to save something from the ruins of their homes. The others had gone to their own places to rescue what they could.

Father went over to Miss Whitlaw. *"You did your best,"* he said.

"But the people."

"I no hear calling in last hour. No one alive left there," Father said.

"Yes," Miss Whitlaw said. *"I guess you're right. My God, I hope you're right."*

The demon boy Miss Whitlaw had sent out came back without a doctor. *"They've declared martial law all over the city,"* he said, wide-eyed with fear. *"And there's a fire to the southeast, a big one, already across Market."* And then he left hurriedly to join his family across the street, salvaging what they could before they fled for safety—though where they were going to go to escape the fire, no one knew as yet.

It was not until months later that we learned how it started. The demons would call it the Ham and Eggs fire: A woman whose house had survived the quake began to make a breakfast of ham and eggs, but the earthquake must have damaged the flue of her chimney, for sparks from the fire caught on the walls, and the whole quarter of wooden houses had gone up in flames. Because the fire companies were off to *Market Street,* there was no real effort to stop it. It was just spreading.

The army came marching in about four hours after

the earthquake. The soldiers had on broadbrim hats with the crown of the hat shaped into a cone. Over their shoulders they wore blanket rolls, in which they had rolled up their belongings so that they looked like they were wearing doughnuts. On their rifles were bayonets. They were headed by an old demon with V stripes on his sleeves that Father said were *sergeant* stripes. The old demon was chewing on a plug of tobacco. *"You'll have to get out of here, ma'am,"* he said. *"There's a fire coming."*

"How much time do we have?"

"Mebbe six to ten hours."

"We have injured here."

"Take them to Golden Gate Park. They'll be safe there. The fire'll be going more north than west."

"I don't see how we're going to get there, sergeant."

He seemed to have sized up Miss Whitlaw and liked what he had seen. *"Now, I'm supposed to keep a lookout for looters and the like, but if I was someone who needed a horse underneath me, I'd try on Van Ness, where I just saw a horse tied to a wagon."*

"But surely there's an owner."

"Yessum. He must have gone back into his house for one too many things, 'cuz the house fell on top of him while he was getting it."

"Thank you, sergeant," Miss Whitlaw said.

"My pleasure, ma'am." He touched the brim of his hat in a kind of a salute. *"Just step lively before the next patrol comes through."*

The Whitlaws and I spent an anxious ten minutes while Father went to get the wagon. We sat down by the front door, clubs in hands, watching for looters. We saw two sleazy individuals, but they took one look at us and slunk on, picking at the rubble as they tried to find something worthwhile to take.

It was a relief to hear the rumble of a wagon and the clatter of hooves, and see Father perched on top of the wagon. We loaded the sick onto the wagon, along with some bedding, some clothes, a frying pan or two, and other things. That plus Miss Whitlaw's bags and our own boxes of possessions took up the wagon. The whole southward side of the city was covered with black smoke now. I could not see the sun, even.

As she climbed onto the wagon beside Father, Miss Whitlaw asked him, *"Don't you want to throw away your club?"*

"Not yet." Father looked grim. *"I no like what I see, come back here."* He did not elaborate, and we did not ask for details.

The streets were strangely empty now. The houses that were standing were tilted every which way, as if they were drunk. Rubble covered the streets. We saw dead horses everywhere, and now and then heard rifle shots. I asked Father what they were, and he replied grimly, *"Soldiers shoot looters."*

Well, we got everyone to *Golden Gate Park,* where there were thousands of other demons and demonesses and their families. Healthy as well as injured, all had taken refuge there. We got our patients to the demon doctors and found a site for a camp, and the demons right next to the site agreed to watch our things. Then we headed back. On her lap Miss Whitlaw now had an antique pistol which had once belonged to her father. She had taken it along in one of her bags as a souvenir, but had gotten it out— just in case we met more than Father's club could handle.

Lefty was waiting for us on the stoop, munching on a chicken drumstick. Father laughed with relief and jumped off the wagon. "Well, you did all right for yourself."

"I might say the same." Lefty looked up at me. "You're both rather filthy, but otherwise intact."

"How about the others?"

"Equally as filthy and equally as intact. Uncle sent me to check on you."

"You can see we'll be all right."

"I also came to get your help," Lefty added. "Uncle won't leave the building."

"The old fool," Father muttered.

"Will you come?" Lefty asked.

"Of course, but let us help our friend first."

Lefty got up then. He had been sitting on a silk napkin that must have belonged to one of his customers. He fastidiously wiped his fingers on the napkin and laid it on his right arm, folding it neatly with his left. Then he slipped it into his pants pocket. "Are you hungry?"

"Can't you hear the rumbling in our stomachs?"

"I thought it was another tremor in the earth."

He produced a big basket of chicken, enough to feed a dozen people. And best of all, a big bottle of rice wine. I suddenly realized how thirsty we were. Father beckoned to the Whitlaws. "*Come on,*" he said. "*It for all.*"

Father helped Miss Whitlaw down, while Robin just jumped. They stood shyly around the basket on their front porch. "*This is* Lefty," Father said.

"*How do you do?*" Miss Whitlaw held out her hand. Lefty took it. Robin's eyes grew wide when she saw the stump of his right hand, and I knew I would have some explaining to do later.

"She does not look very ugly for a demoness," Lefty said to Father. "Most of them do not age well."

Miss Whitlaw smiled politely and looked to Father

to translate.

"He say he pleased to meet you," Father said, hiding a smile. As neither Miss Whitlaw nor Lefty understood one another's language, everything went smoothly.

As we ate, Father asked questions about the Tang people's town in the low voice we all used after the earthquake. It was as if all of us were afraid of attracting the attention of whatever creatures—gods, dragons, or demons had caused the earthquake. Lefty told us about how a bull had appeared suddenly in the streets of the Tang people. He must have wandered up somehow from the stockyards, but many of the Tang people were convinced he was the bull who was one of the four animals who supported the world. The Tang people had surrounded the bull, slapping and shouting and even cutting at him with knives, trying to drive him back to join his brother animals. Finally one stupid Tang man had thrown his knife. It had buried itself deep in the bull's side, and the bull, with a low groan, had staggered on until a policeman had shot it. Many of the Tang people had left after that incident, convinced that the world had become unhinged.

"They may be right," Father grunted, and went on to tell the story to the Whitlaws.

After we finished the meal, we put the rest of Miss Whitlaw's valuables into the wagon. There were her *stereopticon,* her *slides,* her world globe—almost all the essentials of life, Miss Whitlaw said, disregarding food, clothes, and bedding. It was Robin who got out the clothes they would need, and blankets, mattresses, and other things. The wagon was quite full when we finished. Miss Whitlaw arranged a kind of soft nest in the middle of the wagonload. *"And now the window,"* she said.

Father helped her ease it out of the window frame. Lefty let out a low whistle when he saw the window. "Surely it is the very jewel of heaven," he said. We did not need to translate that. Miss Whitlaw beamed. We wrapped it carefully in newspaper and then in a second layer of blankets before we put it in the wagon in the little nest. Miss Whitlaw turned then and took the door key out of her purse. "*Oh, dear, I feel so silly.*"

"*Go on, Auntie,*" Robin said.

"*Who know, maybe they will stop fire,*" Father said, even though he knew they would not. But Miss Whitlaw had been born and raised in that house.

"*Well, when you put it that way,*" Miss Whitlaw said. She walked quickly back up the path to her door and locked it. Then she put the key back into her purse. It was the last time she would be able to do that. Her home would be burned down that night. We started to get onto the wagon with her, but Miss Whitlaw told us to get down. "*Your kinfolk may need help.*"

"*You need help yourself unloading all this and this,*" Father said.

"*I'm sure I'll find some people there to help.*"

"*You sure?*" Father asked.

"*Yes, I'm quite sure.*"

"*You not know how handle horse.*"

"*Who do you think Papa took camping with him?*" Miss Whitlaw took up the reins. "*Don't you worry about us, now.*"

"*You sure you be all right?*"

"*We'll meet in the park,*" Miss Whitlaw said firmly.

"*See you there,*" Father said. We watched until we were sure she could control the horse. The route to the park was clear of holes and rubble in the actual street, so it would not be that much of a problem.

Robin now had the antique pistol, and looked so eager to use it that I was sure she would discourage any would-be thief.

We waited until they were out of sight, and then Lefty turned to us. "She seems nice for a demoness."

"She is a superior woman," Father said.

Chapter 10

Aroused
(April–May, 1906)

The demons we passed had the strangest looks on their faces, too. Once they had been rich and wealthy, and now all they owned were the clothes on their backs and their lives, and they were in danger of losing those too. They looked shocked, as if not quite believing that all of this could happen to them. I could not help remembering what fine houses and mansions had once been there, and what richly dressed demons had eaten and drunk within them. And now they were all gone in less than a minute. The demons we met would have been grateful now for a crust of bread or a cup of water—things they would have turned their backs on just twelve hours ago. I felt very small.

As we walked up the now-deserted streets, Lefty warned us to watch out for demon soldiers. "They shoot anybody they find, because they assume that the person is a looter. But the soldiers are looters themselves. When I was coming here, I saw them drive one family out of their house, and the owners were no sooner out of sight than they broke in and stole everything in sight."

"But the demon soldiers we met were good to us," Father said. "They told us about the wagon."

"That was because you had a demoness with you." Lefty grinned. "From now on, trust to your feet and not to your good fortune."

Once down the hill we saw figures in khaki uniforms moving about. Lefty motioned us away, and we eased back to the top of the hill where we would be out of sight. Then we hid behind a mound of rubble that had once been a house. We spent an anxious half hour there. From down the hill we heard the sound of breaking glass and rough, coarse laughter, and then six demon soldiers walked by, their blanket rolls bulging with loot, valuables tucked into their belts. One demon even had a bushel basket full of trinkets. Their bayonetted rifles were slung over their shoulders, and their very red faces made me think they had been drinking stolen liquor. They were puffing away on fat cigars—I supposed the cigars were stolen too.

It was kind of scary. One day we were living in a law-abiding community and the next day the city and the community had both dissolved, with every person for himself. It struck me that Father and I had probably walked by this house, feeling as safe as we could feel in a demon street, many times, and now here we were hiding behind what was left of it, trying to keep from getting shot.

It was about four in the afternoon when we got to the Tang people's town. The streets were pretty empty. There were more mounds of rubble where some houses had been; others had lost their fronts or sides, revealing their insides like gutted animals. Rats skittered over the rubble, blinking evil red eyes at the harsh sunlight. It felt eerie being in the almost empty streets, for they always hustled and bustled with life at this time of day. Now, except for one or two scurrying people, we saw no one.

Our own Company building had stood up through the quake. The founder had been careful to select a sturdy building that had good wind and water vibrations, a phrase that meant it was in harmony with the rest of the universe. Uncle was standing in the door, a pistol in his hands. One of his sleeves was torn and there was a cut over his eye, but otherwise he was as unchanged as the building. "Well, it's as they say, fools and children have all the luck," he said, but he looked relieved to see us. "So no dragons got you."

Father stopped. "And no dragon would dare shake your house, old man."

"Humph." Uncle turned to me. "You thirsty, boy?"

"Yes, but do you have water?"

"No," Lefty laughed, "only his excellent and venerable collection of wines."

Uncle sighed. "And I think the earthshaking has so disturbed the wines that they'll turn bad."

"We have been drinking since this morning," Lefty said.

"Better save some of that," Father said. "It'll be worth more than gold."

"That's where Hand Clap and White Deer are, seeing it's put away where it'll be safe in the park."

We moved inside the Company building. It was cool and refreshing in there in the shadows. The ironing shelves had been taken down, along with everything else. The only things left were the stove and Uncle's prize chair, looking lonely and forlorn in the center of the empty room. Uncle sat down in it heavily, the pistol still in his hand. He looked even more immovable than the stove or the building. All of us sat down around him on the floor. It was strange to see the air unclouded with steam and not to hear the sound of washing from the back.

"You must have a mound of stuff in the park," Father said.

"No, just the necessities." Uncle shrugged. "Most of it is in *Oakland*." That was the city across the bay from *San Francisco*.

"How did you get it over there?" Father asked.

"On a classmate's boat," Uncle said simply. "Superior men help one another in time of need."

We finished the packing while Uncle supervised us, and by the time we had the last wagonload ready, Hand Clap had come back. Red Rabbit immediately looked for some sugar in my pants pocket, but he had to be satisfied with my promise of some in the future. It had been funny to see Red Rabbit moving speedily—for him—up the street, for like us he did not enjoy being around the rats much. We stopped loading for a moment to listen to the crump crump-crump of cannon.

"They are blasting some of the houses with cannon," Lefty explained. "They are trying to lay a firebreak by blowing up some houses."

"On the way in," Hand Clap added, "I saw them setting dynamite in a drugstore just down the street." He grunted as he hefted a box onto the bed of the wagon. "Going to start around here too. You better come with us."

We all urged Uncle to do it, but Uncle shook his head determinedly. "Someone has to watch this building."

"But there's nothing left to take but your stove and your chair."

"Nonetheless"—Uncle tucked his pistol into his

belt—"the superior man tends his own garden."

At that moment there was a loud explosion that made us all duck, and we saw a huge column of fire and smoke rise over the buildings. Flaming bits of wreckage scattered all over.

Uncle shook his head. "Those fool demons are using too much dynamite. They must have some amateurs on. Why, on the railroads we'd only have used half that charge to blast our way into a mountain."

A moment later we saw plumes of black smoke rise from the Tang people's town. Some of the wreckage must have landed within the Tang people's town and set fire to what buildings still remained fairly intact. It would not be long before most of the Tang people's town, the buildings being almost all of wood, would be on fire.

Uncle planted his feet firmly on the ground and folded his arms across his chest. "I'm staying."

Hand Clap planted his feet just as firmly. "Then I'm staying too," he announced.

"So am I," Lefty said.

"Yes, we'll all stay," Father said.

Uncle glared around at all of us. He was not used to being disobeyed. He scratched his jaw then angrily for some time. Finally he grumbled. "Well, someone with sense better nursemaid the lot of you young rascals. Put my chair on the wagon, but mind you don't scratch it."

Uncle supervised the stowing away of his ancient chair and then sat down on it. He turned around to look at the building for one last time. "It's just as well. That old building was too drafty anyway." But he was fighting back the tears. None of us said anything as Hand Clap clicked his tongue and Red Rabbit jerked the wagon forward.

It was a regular tent city in the park when we finally got there. Cooking fires had spread up and down the park, and lines were forming to get the bread or the tents that the demon soldiers were handing out. Other demon soldiers were busy digging latrines. I found out that the demon soldiers had been doing this all day. So there were some good demons as well as bad ones.

The Tang people had tried to gather into a group. I saw some tents here and there—for the most part, old ones with patches on them, or tents improvised out of sheets. There was a particularly dazzling one of bright purple silk sheets. Father and I both recognized them as sheets that we used to pick up from a demon millionaire. I suppose Hand Clap had picked them up a few days ago and they had been cleaned but not returned. Out of some perverse pride, Uncle had told them to use those sheets for the tent.

White Deer grunted when he saw us. "Good, now one of you can go stand in the bread line." Hand Clap set off with a basket on one arm. We had our own food, but the bread would mean we could make it last longer. We could have the bread for breakfast and lunch if we planned it right. Father, Lefty, and I began to unload the wagon while White Deer started a fire. "Uncle," Father said, "do you think Moon Shadow and I could bring some food over to friends?"

"The only demon food we'll have will be the bread Hand Clap is bringing back," Uncle warned us. "White Deer stocked a good pantry for Tang people, but I don't know if demons would agree."

"They're a big and a little demoness. We've shared some meals together. Anyway, they're not the type to complain."

"One of these days"—Uncle wagged a finger at Father —"you will appeal to my better side once too often and my poor, overburdened, sentimental, soft heart will die of the extra load."

"But till then . . ." Father said with a grin.

"Go on. Go on," Uncle waved us away and went inside the tent.

We found Miss Whitlaw and Robin trying their best to erect a tent. *"Here, let me help,"* Father said.

"Oh, Mr. Lee, *thank goodness you're here,"* Miss Whitlaw said. *"We were so frightened. We heard about the soldiers shooting anyone they found in the streets."*

Father only smiled, and went to work setting up the poles correctly, giving directions to me and Robin. Miss Whitlaw added, *"And you must be hungry,* Moon Shadow. *We saved some bread for you."*

It was like Miss Whitlaw to have saved half of her own meager dinner for her guests. *"No need. We have dinner for you as our guests,"* my father said.

"A real Chinese dinner?" Robin asked.

"Yes," I said.

"Why, how marvelous. You and Robin should go, dear. I'm really feeling quite full." But we suspected the truth. Miss Whitlaw did not want to impose upon her neighbors again and ask them to watch their things. Besides, it was evening and they might want to go to sleep early.

"No need to wait behind," Father said. *"I watch things."*

"But I couldn't—"

"They save me some." And he shoved us all out of the tent.

I was a little afraid then at having to play the host to Robin and Miss Whitlaw; but then I realized that they were probably just as afraid of being my guests. And I thought of what Mother had said. If anyone had been an empress in some former life—at least among demons if not among the Tang people—it was Miss Whitlaw. All the Tang people stared as we made our way among the tents to the sheet tent of the Company. Miss Whitlaw seemed to lose ten years and become sprightlier.

"This reminds me of the circus, Robin," she said as she picked her way over the taut ropes of the tents.

"Except there's no lemonade to drink," Robin said. *"You ever been to a circus, Moon Shadow?"*

"No," I admitted.

"We must take you when all this is over," Miss Whitlaw said, and then paused. We had come into a space where the trees and the tents did not shut out our view of the city to the east. The night sky was a bright fiery red from the fires raging in the city. It did not seem like evening, I realized suddenly, but more like a perpetual sunset. Small white things began to shower down. At first I thought it was snow and got excited, but Miss Whitlaw said the white stuff was ashes. I noticed then that everyone had adopted the hushed voices of the afternoon. There was a strange silence over the camp. People did not look back at the city where their houses had once been.

The Company was waiting inside the tent. They looked a little edgy at having to eat with demons. *"Something smells delicious,"* Miss Whitlaw said.

White Deer looked at me. I translated her words and White Deer grunted, but I could tell he was pleased. And then Miss Whitlaw brought out the universal gift that is cherished in all cultures. From her hamper, which she had carried over her arm, she took out a dusty old bottle. It was of brown glass and the light of the kerosene lamp was reflected in it as if there was a little genie trapped inside. *"This is a bottle of my very own plum brandy,"* Miss Whitlaw said to me. *"Papa used to make it and I never quite got out of the habit, even though I rarely use it—and,"* she added quickly, *"only for medicinal purposes."*

Uncle held the bottle between his hands as if it were a delicate flower. We waited expectantly. He turned the bottle around in his hands and then called for the corkscrew. I got it. Uncle studied the cork and then worked the point into the cork as if he were a diamond cutter. He hated to get bits of cork into the wine. The cork came out with a satisfying pop and Uncle sniffed the bottle. "Delicious," he pronounced. I had a cup all ready for him. He poured some of the rich amber liquid into it. It looked as thick as syrup. He drank about half the cup and smacked his lips. "Delightful," he said and poured another cup for himself. The rest of us tried it. It was sweet and fiery and seemed to settle in your stomach with a warm feeling: like spring was inside you. "Refreshing," Uncle declared, and poured himself a third cup.

Well, anybody who could make *brandy* like that was all right with Uncle. At dinner, he even gave Miss Whitlaw—a woman, and a demoness to boot—the seat of honor in his favorite chair. It was an honor that Uncle might not have given the emperor himself—not even a real emperor of the Tang people, to say nothing of that upstart Manchu one that claimed the throne. We had *forks* out for them, but Miss Whitlaw won extra points by asking Uncle to teach her how to use chopsticks. She took so quickly to them that I was positive that she must have been a Tang woman in another life. Robin, though, stuck to *fork* and knife.

White Deer had done himself proud once again;

not so much for the demons' sake—because he could not have known that we would invite the demons—but because of the Company's honor. There was a kind of salted fish which is delicious with rice. You break off little flakes, because one flake is salty enough to flavor a bite of rice. There were vegetables, including choy, which is a little like the demon broccoli only with yellow flowers. There was barbecued pork, roast pork with an oyster sauce, and cold boiled chicken.

And afterward we finished off the *brandy* and sang a little. Miss Whitlaw sang *"Barbara Allen"* in a high, ethereal voice, with Robin helping her. The Company did not know the words, but the tune itself was lovely, and when I summarized the story for them, the Company all agreed it was a fine song. Then Robin recited a poem—*"The Highwayman"*—which she had learned to act out in school; it was about how a bandit is saved from an ambush of soldiers when his true love blows away half her chest. I can't remember exactly how she does it, but I think she pulls the rifle of one soldier so that it's pointed right at her breast. The surprised soldier pulls the trigger and the noise of the explosion warns her lover away. I helped to translate it and the Company enjoyed it—bandit stories are always popular with us. And for our part, we sang some pleasant songs and acted out some of the stories about Monkey, which we had done once for a guild banquet. All in all, it was a fine evening and we were sorry it had to come to an end.

Three days later, on a Saturday morning, as we were making breakfast, the camp learned that the firefighters had begun to get the upper hand. Where they got the water from I do not know. Maybe they used some of the underground cisterns that had been laid down long ago but had been ignored, or maybe they used saltwater from the bay. Besides, there wasn't that much left of the city to try to protect, now. In any event, we heard that the firefighters were winning. And it was about seven thirty when the rains began.

"Now the rains come," Uncle said disgustedly. He lifted the flap of the sheet to watch it come down.

"We might have had to leave here too," White Deer said. "Things could have gone wrong for the firefighters again, and then nothing would have been saved."

Uncle just snorted, convinced that it was part of the general ineptitude of the deities who were in charge of the universe. He let the flap down. The sheets had already begun to sag on top, and the water ran down into the tent, spattering inside. Uncle sat stubbornly in his chair, opening up his umbrella and holding it over his head. "A superior man," he informed us, "is above such things as getting wet."

"Uncle, how about coming with me to visit Miss Whitlaw?" Father asked. We were all sure that her canvas tent would be drier. And for all of Uncle's pronouncements to the contrary, he was terribly grumbly when he was cold and wet.

Uncle rubbed his elbow. "What for?"

Father pointed to a box of apples that had been sent down from the north from some of our kinsmen. "She might like some of those."

"You take them."

"But they're your apples."

White Deer poked Uncle in the ribs. "Go on. The superior man shares his wealth in adversity." It was White Deer who had to tend Uncle when he had a cold.

"Yes, go on," Hand Clap encouraged. "I'm sure

she'd like the fruit." He probably had the same vision of what it would be like inside the tent if Uncle had a cold. As Hand Clap said, when Uncle sneezed, he made such a noise that he would scare away the Lord of the East Wind, and he was used to noise.

"It might be good to hear a sensible person talk for a change," Uncle observed and stood up. "Come, Moon Shadow, I'll need someone to hold the umbrella."

Uncle splashed majestically through the puddles of water on the ground, slightly hunched over so I could cover him with the umbrella. The Whitlaws were just finishing tea when we came. Miss Whitlaw thanked us for the apples and graciously asked us to sit in her good parlor chairs. Uncle sat down with the stately dignity he could manage when he wanted to. Miss Whitlaw went outside to where someone had rigged a lean-to out of branches to shelter a fire. She brought in some hot water in a teapot to make more tea.

When she had served us, I said, *"Uncle's been all over, Miss Whitlaw. He's even been in the mountains."*

"I there," Uncle said, *"working on Central Pacific."*

"Why, I had a cousin who worked his way west on the Union Pacific," Miss Whitlaw said. *"It was on the other railroad that started from the east. He wrote long letters about it."*

Uncle immediately picked up interest when I translated for him. They launched into a long discussion of their memories, both of railroading and of the *Sierras*. I had no idea the mountains could be so big or so cold or so beautiful. And from there, Miss Whitlaw began asking questions about the Middle Kingdom, and Uncle, given a topic he knew something about, grew even more comfortable. All in all, it wasn't a bad visit. When the rains stopped and Uncle decided it was time to head back—he did not want to dip into their larder by having lunch with them, as Miss Whitlaw urged—we made our good-byes. Going back to our tent, Uncle twirled the now folded umbrella. "When we have the Company set up again, you bring her over for dinner sometime. Then we'll give her a proper dinner."

Sometimes I think there are scales in Heaven, and for every good thing that happens in your life, Heaven balances it with a bad thing. The Company had no sooner warmed to Miss Whitlaw than other demons proved just how malicious they could be. Three days later Father and I were over visiting with Miss Whitlaw when we heard the tramp and clatter of the demon soldiers.

"*In here,*" we heard a voice say.

The tent flap was raised by a young demon officer. One of Miss Whitlaw's demon neighbors was pointing at us. "*Come along, you two,*" the young officer said. "*We're moving you out.*"

"*All of us?*" Father asked incredulously.

"*Just YOU, Chinamen,*" the young officer said. "*You sabe me?*"

Father's hands clenched and unclenched, but behind the young officer we could see a squad of demon soldiers. They were not the same friendly ones who had given out bread and taken care of the refugees. These soldiers all wore the same stern, tense expressions and handled their bayonetted rifles nervously, as if they were in the camp of the enemy.

"*I sabe,*" Father said. "*You must excuse,*" he said to Miss Whitlaw.

"*Well, I don't 'sabe.*'" Miss Whitlaw rose in magnificent outrage. "*How dare you come poking into my tent and commanding my two friends to leave? How dare you tell the Chinese to leave?"*

The officer was taken aback. He became a little less haughty. *"Ma'am, those are the orders. The Chinamen have to go."*

"Why? I daresay they make better neighbors than some other folk whom I won't name because I'm a Christian woman." Miss Whitlaw darted a poisonous glance at the demon who had guided the soldiers over here. The demon shifted uncomfortably on his feet.

"I'm . . . I'm sure, ma'am," the officer said hastily. *"But they've got to go. I'm to take them bound up if necessary."*

Father got up. There was no point getting Miss Whitlaw into trouble too. There was a cast-iron frying pan awfully close to her hand and we now knew just how "forcefully" she could argue. Father picked up our hats. *"Come, Moon Shadow."*

Miss Whitlaw whirled around. *"Surely you're not going. You arrived only a moment ago."*

Father patted Miss Whitlaw on the shoulder. *"It some misunderstanding. We fix,"* he lied, to make her feel better. It was a misunderstanding, but we would not be able to fix it. Nobody short of Heaven could fix it. Father handed me my hat. He fixed his own hat on his head. *"We come back quick."*

"You come back quick as you can, you hear me?" Miss Whitlaw said.

I nodded.

The squad was guarding other Tang people, who stood with their gear on their backs or in wheelbarrows. We were marched through the camp, with demons staring at us, while the soldiers rounded up more and more Tang people. When we got back to the main camp of the Tang people, we found most of the tents already struck. The Company was loading our stuff onto our wagon. There were more soldiers there, standing with rifles at the ready, waiting for some outbreak of rebellion. From the way the demon soldiers acted, you would have thought each of us had a knife up his sleeve.

A long procession of Tang people, many on foot, marched along *Van Ness Avenue* past the gutted mansions of the rich. What the earthquake had not destroyed, the fires had. At the end of *Van Ness,* after several foot-wearying miles, we came to a warehouse. Except for Uncle, myself, and Hand Clap, who rode on the wagon, the rest of the Company had walked. Red Rabbit already had to carry several wagonloads at the same time. Somehow he did it.

But then, the very next day, we were moved to a parade ground at an army fort near the entrance to the bay, the *Golden Gate.* I can't remember everywhere we moved, or when. But I think Thursday morning we were moved to the golf course at the *Presidio,* another army base slightly to the east of the *Golden Gate.* It was as if the demons could not make up their minds. Because it was hard to get fodder for Red Rabbit—the demon soldiers now gave us bread and water reluctantly, let alone fodder for our horse—we sent Hand Clap south with the wagon to some of our kinsmen. Uncle should have gone, for all this moving around was hard on him, but he was needed to help some of the other leaders of the Tang people figure out what to do.

Last year the demon officials of the city had tried to move the Tang people out of our old area to a place called *Hunter's Point* in the southern part of the city, where some Tang fishermen already had a camp. It was now rumored that the demon officials were going to make us rebuild the Tang people's town not in our original location but down at *Hunter's Point;* and yet every other ethnic group in the city was going to be allowed to return to its old homesite.

Friday we were moved back to the parade ground of the fort near the *Golden Gate.* Uncle bore this uncomplainingly, though he was sore all that evening. In true hardship, he could be a source of immense strength. By that Friday, we had dwindled from some twenty-five thousand of us to only a few hundred. Many Tang people had just got disgusted and left for points east, south, and north, where you weren't herded around like a flock of sheep by a shepherd who could not make up his mind. But the few hundred who stayed were the hard core of the Tang people—the stubbornest, orneriest individuals, who were getting tired of being pushed around. Someone had to stand firm.

We pitched our tents—they were quite brown now and no longer a bright purple—for the fourth time in four days. Nobody spoke too much. Father jammed his hands into his pockets, watching White Deer wash the rice. "We let ourselves be pushed around like a bunch of stupid oxen. Why don't we do something?"

White Deer shrugged. "What can we do? They have all the guns."

Father spat contemptuously on the ground. "That's what we always say when there's trouble."

"And what would you do? Take them all on? The superior man rises above such squabbles," White Deer reminded Father.

Father glanced toward the tent where the old, wise heads of the Tang people had gathered to work out some strategy. You could hear their voices rising.

"They sound like a bunch of old hens," Father said.

"They're trying their best." White Deer slammed the lid down on the pot. "What's eating you?"

"I'm sick. I'm sick of greed and stupidity."

"You're just sick of people." White Deer planted his fists on his hips.

"Maybe I am," Father grumbled.

It was very late in the evening when Uncle came back across the grass, looking very tired but smiling grimly. He had had to store away his heavy chair because of all this moving around, so he sat down on an old crate instead; but he did it just as majestically as if it were his throne. He poured himself a cup of tea from the teakettle we had kept boiling all that day. He sipped it while we all sat or stood around, waiting for him to speak. When Uncle finished his tea, he arched his head, grimacing as he scratched the underside of his chin. "I think we have them," he said with a self-satisfied air.

"What magic did we come up with?" White Deer asked.

"It was there all the time, only some of those old fools were afraid to try it. I guess they were afraid of making any kind of trouble." Uncle fished into his pocket and pulled out a handful of coins. He dumped them by White Deer's boots. "There's your magical weapons. There's all the charms and spells you need for these demons. We Tang people own one-third of the land in the Tang people's town outright. For instance, we own the land that our Company was on. The demons can't tell us to move off it if we want to live there. Even they have to follow their own laws. And as for the other two-thirds—well, did you ever stop to think how important we are to the demons? We run a lot of businesses and services that they need. If we were to leave this city completely, their whole economy would be wrecked."

"But we don't want to go," I protested.

"That's not the point, Moon Shadow," Uncle said. "All we have to do is threaten to go. They let us rebuild the Tang people's town in the old place or we go to some city where they'll appreciate us."

"Yes," White Deer agreed, warming to the idea, "some city like *Oakland* or *Los Angeles*. If you name their rival cities, it will make it twice as hard for them to bear."

"That's what we figured."

"It's too bad," Father observed, "that you have to appeal to their sense of greed."

"That's the way it is with demons," Uncle snapped.

"That's the way it is with most men," Father said.

I did not see the meeting that Uncle and some of the elders had with the demons who ran the city. The demons tried to bluster and threaten, but Uncle remained calm throughout it all. He played his hand with a confidence that would have done credit to Lefty when he was gambling. Some of the more stupid demons were inclined to let us go, but some of the others, the men who really ran the city and handled the money, knew that if they lost us, their pocketbooks would be hurting. Their hearts and consciences might be as hard as flint, but their pocketbooks were as sensitive as a cat's whiskers. To make a long story short, we won the same rights that the demon citizens had in rebuilding on their old sites.

We sent out a call then—a call that was heard all around the demon land. Lefty's brother-in-law came down from *Sacramento*. He was a stonemason. White Deer's youngest brother came all the way north by train from *Los Angeles*. He was a carpenter. Hand Clap's young cousin twice removed came all the way from *Colorado*. He had no skills. He just had a strong back, but that was at his elder cousin's disposal. Uncle even got money from some kin and friends in the eastern provinces from whom he had not heard in twenty years. And we were not the only Tang people with kinsmen and friends.

Every day, the men came in by the dozens—dusty, tired men who had journeyed by foot and by wagon when they could not afford a train ticket. They would sit for a moment and stretch out their legs, revealing the holes worn into the soles of their boots. They would be covered from their boots to the crowns of their hats with dust. They would accept a cup of tea with a quiet nod of thanks, and maybe smile and maybe make a joke. And after they had finished their tea, they would pitch right in. They might work sixteen hours a day without pay, expecting only the food they ate and the straw mats they slept on. We were friends and kinsmen in trouble.

The Company's days were filled with a cheerful shouting and singing and swearing and hammering. We were putting up a new building, one made of stone and guaranteed to last a century. It was hard work, but it was exhilarating—the kind of feeling that comes from being alive and taking part in some great common enterprise. Only Father seemed strangely unmoved by the experience. He worked as hard as everyone else, but he did so without spirit. Whenever Uncle talked about building an extra large room for Father to work in, Father always kept very quiet. Finally, four months after the earthquake, Father came by and found me helping to mark off wood for Hand Clap to saw.

"The Whitlaws are leaving today," he said. "I told them we'd say good-bye."

Poor Miss Whitlaw had lost her house in the fire, and so had lost her chief financial support. The money in her cash box was meant to help Robin through college. Miss Whitlaw's land might be worth something once the city was rebuilt, but that meant holding on to it for quite a while. In the meantime, she would have to support herself some other way. Miss Whitlaw had borne her losses with a courage that I had come to expect of her. She had cheerfully taken a job as a housekeeper to some demons over in Oakland across the bay.

I put down the pencil and ruler and followed him without a word. We both washed up silently and put on some clean clothes. As we walked through the city toward the park, we could hear the incessant banging of hammers and the wheezing of saws. Wherever you went, you saw the same wooden frames going up—like the skeletons of houses waiting for their wooden flesh to be attached. It was a city waiting to be reborn.

Father swung his head to the side to avoid being hit by a plank that a hurrying demon carried on his shoulder. He stared after the man. "Look at him. I don't think he's learned anything from the earthquake. He's going to try to make things just like they were—until the next earthquake comes along. And then he'll just build another one."

We walked along for a while. "Houses don't mean much. It's the people inside them that are important," I said.

Father grinned sardonically. "Yes, and you no sooner get to like those people than they're dead, or they move away. Like the Whitlaws."

"But we can meet other people," I pointed out.

Father playfully tipped his hat forward so that it shaded his eyes. "Yes, and you go on losing those new friends that you make just like you lose the new house you build. Don't you want something better, purer, freer in this life?"

"I don't think there is," I said doubtfully.

Father pulled off his hat and smoothed his hair.

"I think an *aeronaut* is free. I think an *aeronaut* may be the freest of all human kind."

"But you don't have an aeroplane."

"I'll build one."

"And how will you live?"

"I'll put on shows and people will pay to see just how pure and free a man can live." He bit his lips thoughtfully. "I think this is my final test, Moon Shadow: the final and truest measure of whether I'm worthy to become a dragon again."

I felt as lonely as I had that first day on the pier, looking at the crowd of strange Tang men. I was not only losing the Whitlaws, but Father as well.

"Why do you always have to change your life just when it looks like you're finally settling in?" I asked.

"Dragons are able to change shape, and so must I. Do you understand?" Father glanced over at me. I dropped my eyes. "Do you, Moon Shadow?" I still did not answer. "Do you?"

"I think Miss Whitlaw may be waiting." I hurried on.

Miss Whitlaw had already folded her tent with the help of some of her neighbors, and carted it off to the temporary army depot. Most of her things had already been stored away in her employers' home. She was wearing a traveling outfit—a long brown skirt with a kind of short cloak of the same material as her skirt. She had on a big hat, which was held to her head by a scarf that she had tied around her chin.

"I'm so glad to see you," she said.

Robin was sitting on a crate, drumming the heels of her high-buttoned shoes against its side. I went over to her. She cocked her head to one side. *"You look even darker than you did before."*

"I've been out in the sun a lot," I said.

"Oh." Suddenly Robin took the book from her lap and thrust it into my hands. *"Here,"* she said. *"It's a gift for you."*

It was *"The Phoenix and the Carpet"* by E. Nesbit.

"It's the closest thing I could find about flying," she explained.

"I don't have anything that nice to give you," I said.

"'S all right," Robin said, pretending to be indifferent. *"I read that book so many times, I got tired of it."*

"All I have is this." I gave her the carving of Monkey that Uncle had given me my first night here. Robin knew what it was, having seen it many times in our stable. By this time, too, I had told her many of the stories about him. *"He likes travelers."*

She turned it admiringly over in her hands. *"Thank you."*

"I got tired of it too." I grinned.

We loaded the two suitcases Miss Whitlaw had onto the wagon and drove them down to the *Ferry Building.* We would arrange to sell her wagon and horse for her. There was always a need for a good horse and wagon over here now with the rebuilding. The whole trip was made in a long silence. In the years we had known them, we had grown probably as close as we could to demons.

We made small talk in the large waiting room of the *Ferry Building,* which had more or less escaped the fire, though they had had to rebuild parts of it. When the ferryboat was ready to leave, the gate, which looked like it belonged on a castle, went up with a rattle of chains. People were getting up all around us, suitcases in hand.

Miss Whitlaw took Father's hand between hers. *"You stay true to your dream, Mr. Lee. I just know that one day I'll be going to a show with your name up on the banner."* Then she turned to me. *"And you keep in touch, you hear, or I will personally walk back across the bay and skin you alive."*

"I guess that goes for me too," said Robin.

"I hear you," I said.

Impulsively, Miss Whitlaw leaned forward and kissed me on the cheek. She was blushing when she stood up again. *"Excuse me for the liberty,* Moon Shadow.*"*

Robin gave me a quick peck and waited defiantly for me to say something but I did not. Miss Whitlaw picked up one of her suitcases. Robin took the other. We waited by the gateway, watching them walk through the dark tunnel out into the bright light where the ferryboat rode the waves. They walked over the gangplank onto its deck. The gate came down with a rattling groan. The sailors cast off the rope and drew in the gangplank, and the water around the ferryboat churned white as the paddle wheels on its sides began to turn.

I did not say much to Father as we rode back to the Tang people's town. What could I say to a man whom I had come to love and respect but who wanted to leave me? That night Father got Uncle alone and I sat down by them. Father turned to me. "Moon Shadow, you once asked me who or what caused the earthquake. I don't know. It could have been the gods, or dragons, or demons, or it could have simply been a natural event. It doesn't matter; supernatural or natural; it means the same: This life is too short to spend it pursuing little things. I have to do what I know I can and must do."

Uncle banged his fist on the arm of his chair. "Not that damn dream again."

"Dream or not, I can fly," Father said matter-of-factly. "I can build a flying machine."

Uncle looked grim. "Even assuming you can build a flying machine and then make money flying it, what will you and your family eat while you're building the machine?"

"It's time I thought of myself," Father asserted.

Uncle was scandalized. "Supposing your father and mother had thought that? Or suppose their fathers and mothers had thought that before?"

"That's cheating." Father sagged in his chair and rested his hands on his knees.

"A superior man admits the truth," Uncle snapped. I could see Father was beat. He hung his head for the longest time, staring down at his hands. I could only think of some immortal who had suddenly woken one morning to find himself in a man's body and realized he was being punished. For the second time in my life, I made an important decision to be with him.

"I want to fly too, Father," I said.

"Stay out of this," Uncle snapped.

"Pardon me, Uncle, but you brought me into this." I looked at Father again. "We should build the flying machine. Maybe you can make a living doing it. And while we're building it, we'll both get jobs. We'll all manage somehow."

Father straightened a little. "Despite what everyone says?"

"A superior man can only do what he's meant to

do," I said.

Uncle laughed scornfully. "Don't give me that nonsense."

"He's the only one I hear talking sense," Father said.

"Don't expect to come back here, either of you," Uncle warned us. He was hurt by our leaving him a second time. "I won't have anything to do with fools."

"Please let me go with you, Father. I won't be any trouble at all, and you'll need help."

Father put his hand on my shoulder. "Yes. I know I'll need help. I was hoping you'd come along."

"Why didn't you ask then?"

"It's not something you can ask."

"Then we'll go together," I said.

Uncle looked at us, both hurt and confused. "Why?" he asked. "Why?"

"It's something we both have to do," I tried to explain, but it was like trying to describe colors to a blind man.

Uncle shoved his chair away from us and got up. "Get away from me," he said.

I was sad about Uncle, but with Father's arm around me, I felt a warm glow inside of me even so. He was Windrider and I was his son.

Chapter 11

Exile
(May, 1906–
September, 1909)

A demon week later, Father and I moved across the bay to a place in the foothills above Oakland. We used Miss Whitlaw's wagon, taking it across on the ferry. Later, Father would return it to the Tang man in San Francisco who had agreed to buy it. The wagon rattled up a dirt path to a plateau halfway up a hillside. The winds roared so loudly about us that Father had to shout to me. "Feel those winds, Moon Shadow?" Father asked. "Aren't they beautiful? They'll help us when we try to launch the flying machine."

I tried my best to hold on to my hat. "Are they like this in the wintertime?"

"I guess so," Father said. "In fact, I hope so. We'll be testing our models every clear day."

I said nothing, because I did not want to spoil Father's enthusiasm. As the wagon rolled on, Father went on making plans. In his own mind, he was already flying. Father took the path that led away from the roadway. Eventually we came to an old iron fence covered with a tangle of weeds and shrubs. I suppose at one time there had been a gate over the path, but someone had taken it away. Father told me that we were living on what had once been a rich estate belonging to the *Esperanza* family.

At first we were surrounded by former orchards of apple, cherry, and apricot trees that had now become wild. I found out later that their fruit was too small and bitter and full of worms to be eaten, but right then the trees filled the air with the sweet promising scent of blossoms. Past the orchards in the middle of the estate was a garden that must have covered nearly ten acres. It seemed as if the garden held every type of flower, bush, herb, and tree in the demon land, but because no gardener watched them they now grew helter-skelter in a riot of color and greenery.

Finally, Father stopped the wagon before two large, ramshackle buildings. I looked at the larger one, which seemed to have once been a mansion constructed in the demon style. "Are we going to live in that?" I asked doubtfully.

"In that old ruin?" Father laughed and pointed out the places on the sides where some scavengers had already taken the boards away. The panes of glass in the windows had been either broken or stolen, and the roof had begun to cave in. Father nodded at the other building, a large one of plain, straight design. It was about two stories high but there were only a few windows at the level of the first story. "No, sir. We're living in the barn."

When we first walked into the barn, the smell nearly knocked me down. Father set down his box of ammonia and disinfectants. I had wondered why he had spent so much money on them, but now I knew. The barn was awfully drafty too, but I guess I ought to be grateful that it was. We scrubbed and soaked and tried almost everything to get rid of the smell of horses and manure, but even after a day's work we did not quite manage it. Disappointed, Father said, "Maybe this will help."

He went over the left wall of the barn where the stablehand had once slept in a little walled-off section. There was a potbellied stove there, and a pipe leading from it to the wall to let out the smoke. There was already a shelf on part of the wall. Father put Uncle's cup of soil there and slipped a dozen incense sticks into it and lit them. Little plumes of smoke, thick as worms, began to writhe in the air. "There," he said, stepping back. "If we can't chase out the smell, maybe we can cover it up."

"Yes, sir." I rolled my sleeves back down after washing my arms and hands. Somehow I knew that the incense would never quite get the smell out. I set a board over two empty boxes and then rummaged around in our things until I found the paper, ink, and inkwell. Then I got some water from the pump outside.

"What are you doing?" Father asked.

"I'm getting things ready for a letter to Mother. We haven't written her yet telling her about our change in plans. The last thing she's heard is that we were in the Tang people's town helping the Company rebuild the store. I thought if we wrote a letter this afternoon, you could mail it when you went back to return the wagon."

Father sat down reluctantly on the dirt floor before the board. "I can just hear the schoolteacher now, telling everyone in the village."

"It's Mother who has to listen to them laughing," I pointed out.

"I wish I could spare her that." Father chewed the end of the brush's wooden handle. "We have the easy part. All we have to do is fly. She has to live in the village." Saying that, he began to write.

Father worked as a handyman or an all-around mechanic when he could, but he would cut firewood or do almost anything so long as it was legal and it paid. I managed to get a job as a delivery boy for a grocer, but it meant I did not talk much with Father. By the time I got home, cooked dinner, and did my lessons and my chores, I would be so tired that I would go right to bed. Eventually I wound up running our household, or maybe our barnhold is a better word. Among other things, I planned our meals, washed our clothes, kept the barn as clean as I could under the circumstances, and oversaw the budget once Father showed me how to do it. That left Father all his free time to work on flying.

Somehow we managed to send some money home too. Once a month, on a Sunday, I walked down into Oakland and rode the *trolley* to the ferry depot, where I would join a lot of other Tang men— houseboys and other dayworkers. From there, we would ride the ferryboat over to San Francisco. Father never went, because he did not want to waste any of his free time.

Once I was in the Tang people's town, I would deposit our money with the district association and pick up letters. Sometimes there were notes from Hand Clap or White Deer (who would convey Lefty's regards, since Lefty himself could no longer write). Then I would finish shopping and start the long trip back home, arriving late in the evening, usually to find Father bent over the table, working feverishly at the plans or finishing some model he was going to test.

I don't know whether the smell of the barn got less or our noses grew used to it, but after a while we stopped noticing it. Spring turned into summer and the grass in the garden changed into a ruddy gold color. When you walked through the orchards, the air was thick with the sickly-sweet smell of fruit rotting on the ground.

It was not until early August that we received a reply from Mother and Grandmother concerning Father's revelations. It was a thick envelope, so I had expected several pages mostly from Grandmother scolding us. But when Father opened it, there was only one single sheet and a second, smaller envelope. He spread the sheet out quickly on the tabletop and began to read out loud. I sat across from him, fiddling with my own writing brush while I listened.

As we expected, Grandmother called Father a fool who was a disgrace to the family, both the living and the dead, and so on. I was surprised that the schoolmaster's brush had not burned up, but she again warned us to watch out for the water in our new demon home, so I suppose she had not totally turned her back on us. As also could be expected, Mother was patient and understanding, saying what a truly wonderful thing it was to meet the Dragon King.

Father picked up the second, smaller envelope and slid it over the table to me. "It's for you," he said, puzzled. I reached over and turned up the light from the kerosene lamp. Sure enough, my name was on it. It was the first time I had ever had a letter addressed only to me.

Father drummed his fingers on the tabletop. "Well, aren't you going to open it?"

"Yes, of course." I hastily tore open the envelope and slipped out the thin rice-paper sheet. I read the letter silently:

It is very hard to say these things by the hand of another. I long to hold you, but the only comfort I can offer are these words which I myself cannot write. But though the words are written by another, they are my words nonetheless.

Above everything else, you must not show this letter to your father, for I must tell you some things about him. First of all, I knew he was an unusual man when I married him, but I had no idea he had once been the physician to the Dragon King himself. I do not care what the others say. I am bursting with pride right now.

But this brings me to the second thing. I wish more than ever that I could be with you right now, for your father has undertaken no small task; but since I cannot be there, you must love him doubly hard. You must give him not only your own support, but also try to give him mine as well.

It is a great deal to ask of you, but I know you will be able to do it. I have not seen you now for four difficult, impossible years, and yet from your letters I feel that you are still the child I love and that you will soon be a man that I can be proud of.

At the bottom of the letter was Mother's name.

I read through the letter several times, feeling suddenly very sad and tired. I had not really thought about my mother in a long time.

"Well," Father demanded impatiently. "What does your mother say? I suppose it must be your mother.

Your grandmother would never waste money on a second letter."

I folded the letter and put it carefully back into its envelope.

"I think she understands, sir, about not telling her your dream and about the delay in bringing her over."

Father pointed at the envelope still in my hands. "Does she say it in there?" He looked as if he were eager to read it.

"No, sir, but that's what she means."

"How do you know?"

"We used to figure out what to put in each one of our letters to you. I know what she'd say and what she wouldn't."

Father massaged his forehead. "How long has it been since I've seen her?" he asked himself. "I think almost twelve years. Why do I want to bother with flying, anyway?"

"White Deer says that you can only follow the course of your own nature." I got up and poured a cup of tea for Father and set it down in front of him. I wished Mother were there. She would have known the right things to say. But as it was, I had to try to stumble through in my own clumsy way. "And who knows? Maybe one of these days we'll fly back across the sea and pick her up."

Father laughed and seemed to relax. "I'm afraid that Hand Clap's more likely to build that kind of machine than me. I'll be happy if I can just stay in the air for a few minutes." But you could tell he felt better. He gulped down the tea. "Well, we'd better be getting back to work."

Then it was fall and the rains came. The trees of the orchard began to lose their leaves and look like sheep huddling against the fence, and new grass and flowers began to shove their way up through the now old and dried-out growths in the garden. When I could, I would spend a lot of time outside, sitting on an old crate by the side of the barn, watching the fog drift in close through the trees, snagging on the branches or crawling catlike through the garden.

It was about the same temperature whether I was inside or outside the barn. We had done our best to repair the holes in the roof, but there were still one or two little leaks that dribbled all the time. We had no spare money to replace the broken panes of glass in the windows, but we did the next best thing by taping some heavy paper over the holes and oiling the paper so it became translucent. It helped cut the wind down some but still let in the light. We had also tried to cover up the spaces between the boards with mud and straw, but even so the wind would get through into the barn. And the place was so huge that we could never quite warm it up. By now Father had hung huge models of the flying machines—some up to six feet in wing span—from the rafters, and these would twist and turn as if they were giant captive moths.

But winter was my favorite time to be outside—on those special days when the rains had stopped and the fog had burned away. The air had been washed clear of any soot or dust or smoke and the whole world seemed fresh and crystal-sharp. I could look out then and see the city of Oakland lying stretched out at the foot of our hill, all the houses looking like toy blocks. And beyond Oakland was the bay, smooth as a pane of green glass. On any sunny day you would see sailboats gliding over the surface, leaving fine white lines behind them that were their wakes. Their sails would belly out full and white before the wind. And the breeze would rise up from the bay, cool and salty, passing over the hissing grass. And beyond the bay was the City—the only city as far as I was concerned. In the next three years, I watched as much of it was restored. The ships would lie at anchor by the wharves like lazy water bugs. You could see the streets tilting skyward and the houses scattered over them like varicolored beads, and the brightest cluster of beads was the Tang people's town. It was as if the earthquake had only been a bad dream.

But if the view in the daylight was good, the view by moonlight was even better. Then all the lights in the houses burned. Below our hill, the lights of Oakland would gleam like a cloud of fireflies and the wrinkling waters of the bay would turn to quicksilver under the moon. And beyond the bay, beyond even the ships with the lights hung on their sides, would be the lights of San Francisco: thousands and thousands of kerosene or gas lamps glittering like the gold scales of a serpent. It was like a river of light, and each light represented a person or maybe several people—the lights of their homes or the streetlights outside them; and I did not think of them as scrabbling for money or being stupid or malicious. It was as if they had each become a tiny star shining in the darkness.

I had found my mountain of gold, after all, and it had not been nuggets but people who had made it up: people like the Company and the Whitlaws. I had not realized until I had left it that I had been on the mountain of gold all that time. And somehow, being on our hillside, I felt above it all now—somehow freer and purer, working toward the fulfillment of Father's dream. Somehow, all the worries and fears of the past seemed small and petty now.

Those next three years were hard years. I was cold sometimes. I was hungry other times. I was tired most of the time. But I could not say I was really unhappy, only uncomfortable. All about me, I had Father's dream taking visible form—first in the pictures and the articles he had taped to the walls, then in the models and diagrams he began to hang up, and finally in the skeleton of the flying machine itself which he began to construct with light wooden poles.

And on three Sundays out of the month, there were trips to the Whitlaws'. At first I had felt sorry for Miss Whitlaw, but I should have realized there was nothing that could faze that lady. She had her stained-glass window carefully wrapped in cloth and brown paper inside a box that Father had built for her. And she always had her *stereopticons* and *slides,* and some of her books.

Some Sundays, though, they would come to visit us and help fly Father's huge model gliders. They were as thrilled at Father's progress as we were. And when we began to actually build the aeroplane, they made a point of coming down with an already fixed cold supper and helping us. But though they called it the aeroplane, or sometimes the flying machine, Father and I always thought of it as Dragonwings.

It took three years to build Dragonwings, because we never seemed to have much money to go around—we were still sending money home to my mother—and because we had to learn by trial and error how to build the frame and stretch the canvas over it. But by the end of the summer of the demon year 1909, we were ready. Father once tried to explain to me just how the aeroplane was supposed to work, but I never did follow much of it, though I do remember the shape.

The aeroplane had no solid body; it was only an

empty frame about twenty feet long, four feet high in front and angling up in back to only about a foot. The canvas-covered wings, which were forty feet long and six and a half feet wide, were on top of the frame's center. Six-foot-long struts separated the top wing from the bottom one.

There was no cockpit, as there is in modern flying machines. The pilot lay flat on his stomach on the bottom wing. To his right, also on the wing, was an engine which powered the two *propellers* by a gear-and-sprocket system like the one on a bicycle. The *propellers* faced to the rear, pushing the aeroplane forward rather than pulling it.

In front of the flying machine was a pair of smaller wings, about four feet long and about a foot apart, which the Wrights called *horizontal rudders*. Future aeronauts would call these little wings elevators, because they forced the aeroplane up and down in the air. The little wings could be tilted upward or downward. When they were aimed upward, they sent the wind at an angle around and through the rest of the aeroplane so the machine would go up. When the front edges were aimed toward the ground, the machine was directed downward. Father handled these with a control held in his right hand.

In the rear of the frame was another set of wings, also about four feet long and a foot apart; but these rose vertically rather than horizontally. The vertical rudders allowed the aeroplane to make a level turn to the left or to the right. But an aeroplane can also turn in another way once it is in the air, and that way is also called *banking*.

As the Wrights wrote Father, *banking* had always been a problem for earlier aeronauts who had tried to do that simply by shifting their weight around inside the aeroplane. The Wrights had solved the problem by controlling the shape of the wings. *Orville* told Father to think of a box from which both ends had been cut and which Father was holding in his hands—his left hand holding the top forward corner and rear lower corner of one end and his right hand holding the top rear corner and the forward lower corner. If Father moved his left hand downward and moved his right hand upward, the top and bottom of the box would twist or warp: The front left edges of the top and bottom of the box would curl downward while the front right edges of the top and bottom would curve upward. If this happened to the two wings of the aeroplane, the two sides of the aeroplane's wings would be presented at different angles to the wind. As a result, the left sides of the wings would rise (and the right sides would dip), flying faster than the right sides, so that the aeroplane would *bank* to the right, that is, the aeroplane would seem to pivot on the right sides of its wings and turn to the right. The wings could be warped in the opposite way, of course, so that the aeroplane would *bank* to the left.

Father built controls for the vertical rudders and the warping mechanism of the wing following the design of the Wrights. Since there was neither seat nor seat belts, Father had to hold on to the flying machine with his left hand. The only way Father could control both the rear rudders and the curving of the wings was with a kind of hip cradle. By moving his hips left or right inside the wooden cradle, he could make the machine turn either left or right; but, of course, he could not make a level turn to the left or right that was separate from *banking* to the left or the right as you can in a modern flying machine. Father's own improvement on the Wrights' original design was to put four wheels on the bottom of the frame's center.

If the flying machine and the control system sound funny, you have to keep in mind that these machines were among the first ever built. It was hard to believe, when you saw a picture of the Wrights' flying machine, that it really could fly. It was mostly a skeleton of wooden poles, with canvas stretched only over the wings. It seemed like a rather flimsy thing to trust your life to, as it was not much better than a big kite.

Our motor was only about twelve horsepower, which we thought very powerful, for in 1903 the Wrights had hunted both in this land and in the other demon lands over the seas for a lightweight engine producing some twelve horsepower, and they had been unable to find one. They had to build their own. Fortunately, engines of the kind we needed were now available, but they were expensive. We had to dip heavily into our savings. And of course the propellers had to be carved exactly according to the Wrights' tables. That was a headache, believe me.

Somehow, we did it. Neither the costs nor the troubles we met building Dragonwings could stop us. Finally there came the day near the end of August when Father announced that we were ready. It was a good thing we finished it when we did, because we were just about broke. We had tried to pay our rent, food, expenses, and money for Mother out of our earnings, but little by little we had had to dip into our savings until we had only enough to pay the rent for next month and hire a team of horses and a wagon to haul Dragonwings up to the top of our hill and fly it. (Even though Dragonwings did have wheels, we needed to carry it in a wagon because its wheels would have sunk into the ruts in the road and its wings, brushing the ground, might have gotten torn or even broken.) If that test flight worked, we'd borrow money somehow and do it a second time, but for an audience of paying spectators. And with the money from that, we'd pay our rent for the next month and hire another team of horses and fly at some county fair near here, and so on.

To be honest, it did not sound like much of a plan to me. Father was more of a mechanical artist than a businessman. He wanted so badly to fly that it never occurred to him that people might not pay to see him fly. Sometimes people want a thing so much that they lose their common sense. But if Father had been practical, he probably would not have been trying to fly in the first place. I shut out all those worries like what would happen if we tested Dragonwings and it did not fly, or how to drum up an audience if Dragonwings did test out.

It was around the end of that same August of 1909 that I began to get jumpy—like I was being watched sometimes from the trees, sometimes from the vacant mansion. At first, I told myself it was just nerves. After all, I was getting positively ancient, for I was now fifteen (or fourteen by demon reckoning). It was not so much my age that bothered me. It was the fact that after six years here in the Land of the Golden Mountain, I had even less chance of seeing Mother.

I was proud of Father for wanting to be a dragon again, and even prouder of the fact that he was now so close to achieving his ambition to fly. I was just sorry that we had not been able to combine his more lofty goals with the more ordinary dream of seeing Mother. Of course, Father thought he could—but even so his scheme had an awful lot of ifs in it. But Mother was patient, so I had to be too.

And the feeling that there was someone or something else around kept on growing inside me.

Sometimes at night when I came back to the barn, I would find a chair where I was sure it had not been, or books misshelved. But with no real definite proof, I held my peace.

On the first Sunday in September, we had the Whitlaws down to help us christen Dragonwings. The night before, Father and I had spent all our time painting scales on the wings, and as an extra touch, Father had painted eyes on two squares of canvas and added them to the front rudders. They hung limp now, but during the flight they would flap like flags.

After they had admired our paint job, Miss Whitlaw produced a small bottle of wine. *"For the christening,"* she said, *"whatever it's to be named."*

"Dragonwings," Father said.

"That's a funny name," Robin said.

"Ah, well, it's a lucky name." Father shrugged. His dream was still something very special and very private, and not to be shared even with the Whitlaws. Robin wrapped both her hands around the neck of the bottle and tapped it lightly on the frame—none of us was very sure about how strong the frame really was. The bottle broke, and Robin ignored the wine stains on her dress to declare in a very solemn voice, *"I christen you Dragonwings."*

But it was mid-September before we could even think of flying Dragonwings. The rains did not clear until that second week of September near the time when we had to pay our rent. The deliveries were light on the sixth day of the week, and after I finished my chores at the store, I was let off early. But when I got home and opened the side door to the barn, I found Black Dog there, rummaging through our bedding.

He sat down on a stool when he saw me. "How do you do, Moon Shadow?"

"What are you doing here?"

"Can't one cousin visit another cousin? It's a lonely country. Maybe I missed the sight of your monkey's face." He bent his elbow and scratched himself like a monkey for a moment. He had always tried to make jokes like that, but they were never very funny. I saw that time had not been very kind to him.

"Do you want some tea before you go?" I asked.

Black Dog smiled coldly. "You have all of my father's charm and tact, do you know that?"

"What do you want?"

He waved a hand at an old overstuffed chair we had found in the mansion and brought into the barn. "Come. Sit and talk with a lonely man." His voice grew hard when I remained standing. "I said sit!"

"I'll stand, if you don't mind."

Black Dog shrugged. He leaned forward and clasped his hands together, resting his elbows on his knees. "We never did get to finish that talk we began a long time ago."

"About what?"

"About those two lovers to whose memory I have consecrated myself."

"You mean the demon dung."

Black Dog laughed and regarded me in a cold shrewd way. "I want you to tell me about the thing you find yourself married to—your life, that is. I want you to tell me why you don't think your life is ugly." He waved a hand around. "You live by yourself with your Father, whom you hardly see. You live in a place unfit even for animals. It is cold in the winter and an oven in the summer. Your clothes are patched. You are undernourished because all your money goes into this demon contraption that you are not even sure will work. And you don't think your life is ugly?"

"What do clothes or food or a house mean?" I shrugged. Suddenly I realized something. "You're jealous, aren't you? You're jealous that we have something to believe in."

Black Dog stopped scratching his leg and slipped his hand into his boot. He pulled out a knife. "I'd like you to find the beauty in my cutting off your nose and ears." He got up slowly. He was smiling to himself. "Yes, I'd like you to try to tell people how beautiful you are with only a stub of a tongue."

I grabbed the nearest thing to hand. It was one of Father's books. I threw it at Black Dog, but he ducked. He came toward me slowly, the knife gleaming in his hand. I turned and darted out the door. Black Dog was right behind me. I could hear his boots pounding the ground. I ran through the tall flowers in the garden and made it into the orchard. I wanted to take a shortcut through the orchard to the road leading down to the town, but then my foot caught in a root. I fell forward into the weeds and old leaves. I got up on my hands and knees and caught Black Dog's boot in my ribs. I toppled over onto my back. He drove a knee hard into my stomach. "Or maybe I'll take a testicle or two."

He let up on my stomach a bit so I could breathe. I suppose he wanted me to get enough air so I could beg; but I suddenly got sick of the whole cat-and-mouse game. "Go on," I told him. "Get it over with, then."

"You won't be singing that tune the first time the knife breaks your precious skin." When I did not say anything, Black Dog smiled. "Well, you're a plucky lad, though you're a fool. I'll let you off easily if you tell me where you keep your money."

"No."

He jabbed his knee into my stomach and pressed

the knife point against my throat. "Come on. Come on. Tell me where the money is. You just said yourself that money wasn't important."

"Dragonwings is."

We heard a branch snap then. Black Dog did not look around. He kept the knife to my throat. I felt my throat muscles begin to tighten as if they were trying to crawl away from the point. "Don't take another step," Black Dog warned. "I can cut your son's throat before you can jump me."

"Don't harm him," Father said.

I heard him walk around from behind us until he stood in front of Black Dog.

"How important is that demon contraption to you?" Black Dog asked.

"It's very important."

"More important than your son's life?"

"Don't tell him, Father," I said.

"No," Father said. "I'll get the money for you."

"Father, don't."

But I saw Father walk over to a nearby oak tree. An old, battered birdhouse swung from one of its branches. Father reached up. Even he had to stand on tiptoe to get it. He took it down and pulled off the roof top—it was only tacked on lightly with very small nails. He took the money out—a thin roll of demon dollar bills and tossed the birdhouse down. He put the bills into his big handkerchief and tied up the corners into a bundle. Then he tossed it over to Black Dog. Black Dog snatched it up like a hungry dog after a bone. He stuffed it into his pockets.

"I should slit your son's throat anyway."

"And you know I'd never rest till I got even with you."

"Yes, I respect you at least that much." Black Dog got up and ran off into the trees. I started to get up to chase him but felt suddenly dizzy. I must have banged my head when I fell. And my chest where he had kicked me felt suddenly tight. I fell forward. "Moon Shadow," Father said. He bent over me.

"Go after him," I said. "That *bastard*. That *son of a bitch*."

"He's still our cousin, despite what Uncle did," Father said sternly. He helped me back into the stable and brewed some tea. Father poured a cup for me from the teapot and gave it to me. I drank it. Outside, I could hear the rain.

"I'm sorry you had to tell him."

Father patted my arm and managed a smile. "It doesn't matter. I'm going down to report this to the *sheriff* now."

"Do you think it might do any good?"

"It might." Father grinned and shrugged. "And it might not."

It was getting near sunset now. I could see the red light within the barn. Our rent money had been in that roll, as well as the money we had planned to use for renting a wagon and a team of horses. What we were going to do for money, I didn't know.

Well, the *sheriff* never did catch Black Dog. And the next day when the landlord came around for his rent, he got mad at Father when Father asked him for an extension. He gave us three days to come up with the money or he'd claim everything inside the place. But we didn't know anybody in the town we could borrow money from. They all thought of Father as the *Crazy Chinaman*. We knew beforehand that Miss Whitlaw did not have any money she could lend out, for Robin's college money was sacred and untouchable even if we were inclined to ask. And Father was too proud to go back to the Company.

We had to go, but how? Dragonwings was too big

to be carried on our backs and we had no money to hire a wagon. We tried all the next day, but no one would rent us one on credit—not to the *Crazy Chinaman*. Even my employer in the store refused, saying it was too much money. It looked like we were stuck. We would be able to take away only what we could carry. We were going to lose our Dragonwings.

Father did not say anything when I put on my boots and hat and went down to the town through the rain to use the store's electric talker, or *telephone*, as the demons called it. I wound the crank with a whirring sound, and when the operator came on, I gave her the number of the house where the Whitlaws worked.

"*Why hello*, Moon Shadow," Miss Whitlaw said. "*How are you?*"

"*Fine. I'm afraid you won't be able to come down tomorrow. We're . . . we're moving.*"

"*Oh? Found a better place?*"

"*Yes, that's it.*"

"*Well, let us give you a hand.*"

"*No, no. I couldn't think of it.*"

"*Nonsense, there's always work to be done. Expect us there right after church.*"

"*No please, you mustn't come,*" I said desperately.

There was a pause at the other end of the line. "*Is there something wrong?*" she finally asked.

"*No, no. Everything's just fine.*"

"*Well, then, why can't we come over?*" she demanded.

"*We'll just be busy.*"

"*So busy you don't need help?*" Miss Whitlaw asked suspiciously.

"*Yes, that's it,*" I said, and hung up before she could ask me anything else.

The rain had stopped by the time I got back. I

could not make out where Father was in the barn when I first got back. Then I made out a shadowy figure sitting near Dragonwings.

"Father?"

He stirred in his corner. I heard a groping at the stove, and then he struck a match and the light flared about his face as he bent over the kerosene lamp, intent on lighting it. He shook the match out and then trimmed the flame. Then and only then did he look up. He fumbled painfully for the right words. "It's finished," he finally said.

"We still have a day to raise the money," I said grimly.

"You will not go to Uncle," Father said. He ran his hand lightly along the lower wing. He stood up suddenly and got his padded jacket from the nail on the wall. He put it on silently and gestured to me to accompany him. Outside, the night was a cool, crisp autumn evening. The rain had just washed everything, seeming to sharpen the plants' smells. The colors seemed brighter, and the beaded raindrops gleamed like jewels on the petals of the flowers and the leaves of the trees. It was clear for the moment, but I could see the fog beginning to move over San Francisco.

I could not see how people could stand to live in the flatlands when they could live in the hills. There is something about the view from the hill that is exciting—a kind of godlike perspective in which men become only tiny creatures walking about their toy houses on a patch of land which seems to float on a vast ocean under an even bigger sky.

Father started to trudge up the hill. I had to run to catch up with him. The road was muddy and our boots made wet, sucking noises. My jacket was not really thick enough to hold out the wind, and I pulled the collar tighter about my neck. It was a cold, sharp wind, but with a salt-sea smell. Father glanced at me, but still he said nothing. The setting sun behind us cast long shadows, which raced up and up ahead of us along the road.

And then at the very top of the hill we turned off, walking to the very edge of it and looking down on the barn below us. Father crossed his arms, slipping his hands into his armpits to keep them warm. "So this is the way it ends," he said finally. "We came so close and yet we failed."

The fog had completely covered San Francisco now and was rolling over the bay toward Oakland. It was as if the world below us were slowly fading away like the dream it was, and only we existed now on a tiny island of reality here on this hilltop.

"Maybe this is the final test in this life," I suggested hopefully.

Father thought for a bit and laughed. "Yes, maybe it is."

"We can build another Dragonwings. You have your designs now, and we know all the tricks of actually building an aeroplane."

Father grunted, and he smiled in his old way. Then he tilted back his head and began to sing:

> There is a little beauty
> In the op'ning of a flower.
> There is a little glory,
> Though it only lasts an hour.
>
> There is a little sorrow
> In the final farewell kiss.
> There's only a little pain
> Though you'll never again see your miss.

I have a little dream
For the flying of a plane.
I have a little scheme,
I'll follow yet again.

There is a little heaven,
Just around the hill.
I haven't seen it for a long time,
But I know it's waiting still.

Then he clapped his hand on my shoulder. "How about a cup of tea to warm our old bones?" he asked. Poor Black Dog: There was some beauty to life after all, even if it was only the beauty of hope.

Chapter 12

Dragonwings
(September, 1909– June, 1910)

I do not know when I fell asleep, but it was already way past sunrise when I woke up. The light crept through the cracks in the walls and under the shutters and seemed to delight especially in dancing on my eyes. Father lay huddled, rolled up in his blanket. He did not move when the knock came at our door. I was still in my clothes because it was cold. I crawled out of the blankets and opened the side door.

The fog lay low on the hill. Tendrils drifted in through the open doorway. At first I could not see anything but shadows, and then a sudden breeze whipped the fog away from the front of our barn. Hand Clap stood there as if he had appeared by magic. He bowed.

"There you are." He turned and called over his shoulder. "Hey, everybody, they're here."

I heard the clink of harness and the rattle of an old wagon trying to follow the ruts in the road. Toiling up the hill out of the fog was Red Rabbit, and behind him I saw Uncle on the wagon seat. The rest of the wagon was empty—I suppose to give Red Rabbit less of a load to pull. Behind the wagon came the Company, with coils of ropes over their shoulders and baskets of food. I ran down the hill, my feet pounding against the hard, damp earth. I got up on the seat and almost bowled Uncle over. For once Uncle did not worry about his dignity but caught me up and returned my hug.

"Ouch," he said, and pushed me away. He patted himself lightly on his chest. "I'm not as young as I used to be."

Then Hand Clap, Lefty, and White Deer crowded around.

"Am I ever glad you're here," I said. "Poor Father— "

Uncle held up his hands. "We know. That's why we came."

"But how? Why?" I was bursting with a dozen questions all at once.

"Why, to help you get that thing up to the top of the hill," Uncle said. "Why else would we close up our shop and take a boat and climb this abominable hill, all on the coldest, wettest day ever known since creation?"

"But you don't believe in flying machines."

"I still don't," Uncle said sternly. "But I still feel as if I owe you something for what was done to you by that man who once was my son. I'll be there to haul your machine up the hill, and I'll be there to haul it back down when it doesn't fly."

"We were all getting fat anyway," White Deer said, "especially Uncle."

"It might be easier to rent a team of horses and a wagon from a demon," I warned.

"Who wants their wagons and their lazy horses?"

Uncle asked airily.

"But you have only one horse and we'll need a team."

Uncle swept his hand around at the Company. "When a lot of the demons' fathers were too lazy to work their mines, we took those mines over and made them pay by the sweat of our brows and the ache in our backs. And when the demons were too scared to go into the mountains to build the paths for their trains, we went and dug up whole mountains. Between Red Rabbit and us, we'll carry your flying machine to Heaven and back if we have to. Call it our penance. We don't want to come back in our next lives as dogs because we felt no shame." Uncle held me off at arm's length. "But look how tall you've grown."

"And how thin," White Deer said.

"And ragged." Lefty fingered a patch on my pants.

"We've been doing all right," I insisted.

"Well, you haven't starved to death or broken your necks," Uncle observed, "which was more than I ever expected. Now." He clapped his hands together. "Come, I'm getting cold."

We helped Uncle down from the wagon. "Wait outside for a moment," Uncle said to the others. We went into the barn. Uncle planted his fists on his hips and looked around. "By the magic hairs of Monkey's tail, you've been living in this smelly, drafty place?"

"For the last three years."

"You're both crazier than I thought." Uncle pointed up at the large, dark shapes of the glider models, turning on their strings. "What are those?"

"Models of Dragonwings." I pointed at our flying machine.

"For a moment, I thought the thing had whelped." Father sat up, blinking sleepily. Uncle and I walked over to the stove. Uncle coughed politely, and when he saw him, Father jumped to his feet and began to brush some of the dirt from his shirt. Uncle took off his hat, inspecting the wall for dust first before he hung it on a nail.

"I didn't know you were going to come," Father said.

"Of course, you didn't. Neither did I until last night, and how were we supposed to get word to you when you live off in the wilds?"

"It's only the foothills, Uncle."

"It might just as well be in the wilds." Uncle walked past Father, ducked under some models and, slipping between the wall and the wing, eyed Dragonwings critically. "How will that thing ever carry you?"

"It's quite capable of carrying my weight." Father came forward eagerly to point at the motor. "Provided that the motor can move me through the air at a certain speed."

Uncle put his hands delicately to his forehead. "Don't try to explain. I understand what you're saying now less than if you told me the Buddha came down and picked it up and hopped around the hills with it."

"If you just came to laugh—" Father began, bristling.

"I came to help," Uncle snapped. "Not because I believe in your crazy dream. Call it an old man's whim if you like." But then Uncle relented for a moment. "And we didn't come to laugh. There will be those among the Tang people who will laugh—but now they will have to laugh at all of us, for we'll share in your folly."

"All of them, Father," I said. "All the Company came."

Father turned now to see the silent, smiling

Company in the doorway. Father scratched the back of his head and then grinned. "Well, don't just stand there, boy. Get the water boiling for tea. Lots of water."

We sat in the dirt or on the mats near the stove. Father used firewood lavishly and we shared around the meat dumplings and cups of steaming tea. "Well, we'll get to see Dragonwings fly once before we lose it," Father said with a laugh.

"Don't worry about losing it either," Uncle said. "We'll give you the money to pay your rent too. Call it a loan, a compensation." He wagged a finger at Father. "And don't give me any pigheaded reasons why you can't take it. Pride's always been the great sin of our family."

"Look on it as an act of charity to accept our money," White Deer said. "It would make us all feel much better."

Father considered that for a moment. He set down his cup and looked around with a smile. "It's not a shameful thing to take money from friends, and you are my friends. I thought I ought to go it alone with just my son, but I was wrong. I'll own up to it."

"Good," Uncle said. "Because we dropped the money off on the way up."

"But how did you know the amount, or where my landlord lived?" Father asked. "And how—"

"We have our ways," Uncle said with a secret smile. "Now show the others this magnificent machine that's about to carry you to the moon." The others all walked around Dragonwings while Father explained things between bites of meat dumpling, trying to convert the jargon of aeronauts into common speech.

It was not until two hours later that we got to start. Father threw off the crossbar and swung the wide barn doors open. We hardly ever used them, using the normal-sized side door instead, so the barn doors creaked on their hinges as if reluctant to open. The sun had burned through the fog by that time. It looked as if it were going to be a hot day later.

Hand Clap backed the wagon into the barn, and we put the tailgate down and propped some boards against the wagon bed so we could use them like a ramp. Then, using a system of ropes and pulleys hung from the rafters, we hauled Dragonwings onto the wagon bed. I could only compare the heavy weight of Dragonwings to the light pair of wings that Father had worn during his visit to the dragon kingdom. The magic of this land only imperfectly captured the magic of the dragons.

Gently, coaxingly, Hand Clap made Red Rabbit head out of the stable. For the first time, Dragonwings emerged out into the open world. Father pointed up the hill. "We'll go to the very top."

Uncle looked dubiously up the steeply inclined hill. "This hill," he noted, "is a very steep hill."

"If you're feeling too old, you can stay here," White Deer said.

"No, no," Uncle glared at White Deer. "I can still climb. I was only thinking of you, old man."

"Maybe Uncle has a point," Hand Clap said. "Maybe a less steep hill . . ."

"No." Father finished lashing Dragonwings to the bed of the wagon and jumped down. "It has to be this one. The winds are right."

"Ah, well, it's the winds, old man," White Deer said.

"Maybe we'd better hire a team of horses," Father said to Uncle.

"Didn't I say the Company would take your machine up to the hilltop!" Uncle said. It would have made much more sense to have hired a team or even two teams of horses, but it was a point of honor now with Uncle for the Company itself to take the flying machine up to the hilltop. And perhaps Uncle wanted to make up to us for all the time we had been living out here like this, trying to prove he was wrong about our never being able to fly. Uncle added, "I'll get your machine up to the top of the hill if I have to carry it on just my back."

White Deer slapped Father on the arm. "No use arguing with the old man." White Deer lifted a coil of rope out of the wagon, laid his arm through it, and went to the front of the wagon to begin tying lines there. We would pull alongside Red Rabbit.

When everything was ready, we took our places. Hand Clap was on the wagon seat because Red Rabbit was most used to him now. White Deer and Uncle were on Red Rabbit's left on one rope. Father and I were on another on Red Rabbit's right. Lefty would push from behind.

White Deer tied the rope around his waist.

"You sure you want to do that?" Father asked. "Supposing Red Rabbit panics."

White Deer tested the line. "I could outrun even a panicked Red Rabbit. He's almost as old as Uncle, you know."

"No one," Uncle declared, "is as old as me."

Uncle took his place behind White Deer, and Father made me get in front of him near Red Rabbit's head— just in case Red Rabbit panicked anyway.

"Ready?" Father asked.

The Company chorused they were.

"Then let's go," Father said.

"Heeyah," Hand Clap shouted. He cracked the reins against Red Rabbit's rump and he started forward. We paced along beside him, passing through the garden and the orchards. Father and I had cleared away any brush or trees on either side of the path that might have hurt Dragonwings. We had even taken down the gate and part of the fence on either side, just to make sure Dragonwings would pass through safely. But when Hand Clap swung the wagon onto the road leading to the top of the hill, Red Rabbit balked. "Come on, come on," Hand Clap shouted. He shook the reins over and over.

I had slipped a cube of sugar into my pants pocket before we left. I took it out now and offered it to Red Rabbit. He sniffed it and then his great yellowed teeth closed over it delicately. I felt his warm, moist breath blow on my wrist. He wanted more. His ears shook ingratiatingly. "I'll give you more," I whispered, "after we've gone to the top of the hill and back." I took one hand off the rope to stroke his nose. "Please, Red Rabbit. I know it's asking a lot, but please pull. Pull as you've never pulled before."

Red Rabbit swung his head back to the road and leaned forward against the harness.

"Now help Red Rabbit," Uncle called.

We strained at the ropes. I stumbled and got up. I stamped at the ground this time, getting better footing. Slowly, ever so slowly the wagon began to creep up the hill. The ropes burned at my hands so that the rope fibers seemed to brand my skin. And Dragonwings, its wings waving over either side of the wagon, lurched forward. Foot by foot, we pushed and pulled the wagon with Dragonwings up the hill, its wings dipping and bobbing as if it were tensing itself.

"Easy, easy," Father called anxiously from the side. He was afraid of the wings breaking.

And for one moment I hated Dragonwings, for as light as we had tried to make it, it was still very heavy for only one old horse and several men and a boy. And I hated Dragonwings, not for what it had cost both my parents and me, but just for being so fat and heavy. I was beginning to be afraid for Father when he tried to fly in it.

Uncle began a chant that the Tang men had used nearly forty years ago when they were building the paths for the demons' trains. And the rest of us, hauling in rhythm to his chant, began to find it was easier. I would say, too, that Uncle pulled the hardest of any of us. And all of a sudden I saw that if life seems awfully petty most of the time, every now and then there is something noble and beautiful and almost pure that lifts us suddenly out of the pettiness and lets us share in it a little. It did not matter whether Father flew or not. It was enough that the Company had come.

I do not know how, but we managed to get Dragonwings to the top of the hill. For a long time, nobody said anything. We were all too busy trying to get back our wind. It was a good time, too, just to admire the view, each man with his own thoughts as he looked out at the great sweep of bay. The winds began rising from the bay waters, racing over Oakland and sweeping low over the hissing weeds, which nodded back and forth in great shimmering waves of gold. Father buttoned up his coat against the chill.

"The horoscope book said this is a most auspicious day," he told Uncle. "I looked it up before we left. I think the book was right. Just feel those winds."

"The book better be," Uncle said, "or the only one who will enjoy this day will be the mortician."

Lefty had sat off a ways on top of his coat, which he had spread over a rock. He shaded his eyes.

"Someone is coming," he called.

We saw the heavily clothed figures tromp up the hill. Miss Whitlaw's face lit up when she saw all of us gathered on the top. *"Thank goodness,"* she puffed. *"I thought we were going to be late."* Beside her, helping to support her arm, was Robin, also coated, scarfed, and booted against the cold damp of the morning. I suppose they figured to shed everything when it got hot later.

Father came down the road and took Miss Whitlaw's other arm. *"How you know we flying?"*

"Oh," Miss Whitlaw said gaily, and glanced at Uncle, *"a little birdie told me."*

"Did you tell them?" Father demanded of me.

"No, sir. I kept my promise. I don't know how they found out, but what does that matter? Your flying is as much theirs now as it is yours."

Father stood for a moment with his hand on Miss Whitlaw's elbow, but finally he grunted. "I guess it is."

Miss Whitlaw had not understood our conversation, but she could get the meaning of it just from Father's angry tone. *"Now you just blame a snoopy old lady, Mr. Lee. I just had to know what was wrong, so I had my employer, who knows your landlord, call him and find out what was the matter. And then I got hold of your friend, Mr. Deerfoot, over in the City, and he gave a message to your Uncle for him to call me up."*

"You actually used an electric talker?" Father asked Uncle in disbelief.

"I'll admit that they can be convenient." Uncle shrugged.

"And so we worked out everything between us," Miss Whitlaw said.

Father grinned down at Robin. *"It good thing you*

got here. I wonder how we going to fly without one of my helpers here."

We untied Dragonwings then and eased it down the ramp by sheer muscle power. Then, lifting, pulling, and pushing, we rolled it to the crest of the hill.

Robin tapped one big, bulging coat pocket. *"We brought a cordial to warm you."* She slid a large bottle out of her pocket.

"That very, very thoughtful," Father said. He uncorked the bottle and took a sip. "Now that's a righteous wine." He passed it to Uncle. "Here, old man, this should drive the chill out of your bones."

Uncle sipped the cordial. "I'll race you round the hill and back again."

He handed the bottle on to the rest of the Company. Even Robin and I got a sip. Then Father clapped his hands together nervously. *"Well, it time to start."* With a nod to Robin and me, he headed for Dragonwings.

Father had left about thirty feet between Dragonwings and the crest of the hill where it sloped sharply for some hundred feet before opening on the ruin of the *Esperanza* estate and our barn. And then the hill dipped sharply again until it came to rest in the flatlands below. We all marched around in the area in front of Dragonwings, tramping the weeds down so the ground would be fairly level. Then Father coiled up his queue into a tight bun behind his head and pinned it there.

Robin took her place before the left propeller with her hands resting on the blade. I took my place beside the right propeller. Father himself lay belly-down on the bottom wing. With his left hand he grabbed hold of the frame. With his right, he took the front rudder controls. He pulled back on the controls and the front rudders tilted upward. He pushed forward and they tilted downward. Then Father shifted his hips to the left. The rear vertical rudders twisted to the left and the wings curled slightly, as if they were alive. Father shifted his hips suddenly to the right and the rudders shifted to the right and the wings warped again. Father straightened the front and rear rudders and the wings again. The wind drummed at the canvas over the wings. The sky seemed alive and waiting.

"*All right,* Moon Shadow, *Robin,*" Father said. We both pulled down at the propellers and backed away. The motor beside Father coughed into life, turned over, and caught. The bicycle chains clinked musically as they turned the propellers. The wings began to vibrate, and you could feel the life begin to course through Dragonwings. Robin stepped back and I ran around behind Dragonwings to join her. We were both exhilarated in the wind from the propellers, which rippled across the grass. Suddenly the wind had competition here on the hilltop. The flags on the front rudders stiffened, and we could now see the eyes painted on the flags. It was as if Dragonwings had finally woken.

Dragonwings lurched forward, bumped, stopped, and lurched forward again, like some great lumbering beast coughing to itself as it got up out of bed. Father gripped the frame of the wing tightly with his left hand and pulled back sharply with his right, so that the front rudders angled skyward. Dragonwings rolled toward the steeply slanting hillside. The wooden wheels made crisp, crunching sounds as they crushed the weeds. Dragonwings seemed to teeter for a moment, balancing on the very edge of the hillside. I wondered if Dragonwings were simply going to roll down the hill. Robin crossed her fingers. Silently, I asked Grandfather to help us.

Suddenly the wind blew even harder up the hillside. The grass all over the hill hissed even louder, like one giant snake. The nose of Dragonwings suddenly tilted up like some bird scenting the wind that would carry it home. The wind roared over the hilltop, seeming to gather beneath the wings. The canvas of the wings bellied upward, taut and swollen and eager. Dragonwings seemed to leap into the air about five feet and hang suspended. I held my breath. I saw Father twist his hips to the right, and the wings began to curl and the rear rudder curved to the right. Slowly, ever so slowly, Father began to bank in that direction. He had controlled his flight! He was free in the sky.

Everyone cheered spontaneously. Father turned in a leisurely circle over the hilltop, coming back toward us. In his traces, Red Rabbit stamped and snorted, so that Hand Clap had to run over and quiet him down. I raced along beside Dragonwings for a moment, my legs pumping, my head dizzy, my heart filled with pride. "Father, you did it. You did it."

Father turned his head. There were a few strands of hair that had slipped down over his eyes, but the wind of his passage blew them away from his face again. He grinned and winked. And then he passed me. His wings brushed the grasstops and then the left side of his wings dipped dangerously toward the ground, but he steadied Dragonwings with a shove of his hips. Dragonwings rose into the air as Father completed his circle and headed down the hillside toward the bay.

I plunged down the slope after him. I could hear the others pounding behind me. Robin shouted for me to wait, but I ignored her. My momentum carried me recklessly forward. Once I nearly fell, but I caught myself with my hands and scrambled on. By the time we had reached the bottom, where the garden stood along with our stable, Father had already reached the road that marked the end of the *Esperanza* property; he began to turn back over the orchards toward the garden. He was flying as high as twenty feet now, and the sun, gleaming through the painted canvas, made the wings seem like living flesh. It was as if he were no longer a man, but truly a dragon again.

We watched him fly for perhaps four minutes around the *Esperanza* estate while we stood knee-deep among the flowers.

"Look at him," Uncle shouted. He was as excited as a little boy. "Look at him. Just look."

"But how is he to come down?" Lefty asked.

Uncle laughed. "Tell this man how he is to come down."

"He'll land back on the hilltop." I added, "More or less."

"More or less?" Uncle asked, puzzled.

"We hope without cracking up the flying machine."

"Oh," was all that Uncle said. He began scratching anxiously at the back of his neck. "Whom do you ask to help an aeronaut? The winds? The dragons?"

"All of them," White Deer said.

But we never did get to see whether Father would land all right or not.

Father had just completed another circuit of the estate and was banking to the left over the fences, so his nose at the time was pointed toward the hillside. I heard a shrill, high, singing sound as the bolt that held the right propeller to the frame snapped. Horrified, I saw the propeller spinning away from

Dragonwings in a lazy arc. The right side dipped dangerously. Father cut the motor and twisted the rear rudder hard to the left, tilting the front rudders upward so that the wind lifted the right side even more. Dragonwings straightened itself. It was deadly silent now in the garden. Father told me later that he had hoped to glide to a landing. But by now he had come too close to the hillside. I saw him twist violently to the left in his hip cradle, trying to turn even farther to the left, away from the hill. Too late.

The next moment seemed to take forever. I watched helplessly as Dragonwings started to turn, but the right side of its wings brushed the hillside. The wooden frame of the right wings snapped in a dozen places. Broken wooden poles ripped through the canvas as it flapped upward. The left wings rose leisurely until they were almost straight up, and then Dragonwings leaned forward and burrowed nose first into the hillside. The body of Dragonwings swung back and forth drunkenly and then hung at an odd angle.

I raced toward Dragonwings, feeling as if I had been betrayed. Somehow, after we had lavished so much time and effort and money on it, it should never have let one of its bolts snap and destroy itself and maybe kill Father. Father had been thrown clear of Dragonwings and lay on his back. I took his wrist. He still had a pulse.

Puffing, Uncle joined me. It was surprising that he could run at all, let alone outdistance the others. It must have been as Uncle always said: There was a lot of life still left in his old beat-up body. Uncle dropped to his knees beside me and, with delicate hands, felt Father's bones. The others gathered around, catching their breaths. Finally Uncle straightened and looked around, relieved. "I think his right leg is broken and maybe two of his right ribs. That's all."

"You mean he'll live?" I asked.

"For now, yes, until he tries his next flying machine." Uncle shook his head.

"What did he say? What did he say?" Robin demanded.

"Father's all right," I said.

We cannibalized Dragonwings to make a stretcher for Father out of the wooden poles and canvas. Uncle and White Deer set his leg—there was plenty of wood for that—and we bound up his sides tight with some old lengths of cloth. Miss Whitlaw sent Robin after a demon doctor. By the time she got back with one, Hand Clap had gotten the wagon down from the top of the hill and driven it into the meadow. We had lifted Father onto the wagon and taken him straight into the stable. Uncle had also sent the Company back to the hillside to clean up the wreckage, so it was all piled into the wagon. That way there would be no embarrassing questions to have to answer.

After the doctor left, we waited for Father to wake up. To occupy ourselves we made pots and pots of tea. *"I wish,"* Miss Whitlaw said as she sipped her tea, *"that I had never had my employer begin making inquiries."*

"I don't think Father would have wanted it any other way." I added, *"Neither do I. It . . . it just had to be."*

Father stirred then and groaned and sat up, leaning on his elbows. He winced and looked at his sides. "What's broken?"

"Only a leg and some ribs, no thanks to you," Uncle snapped. "It could have been your head or your back, you know."

"Yes."

I got some tea for Father. "Dragonwings is a wreck. We'll have to build another one."

Father sipped his tea and set the cup down carefully on the dirt floor. "Would you be disappointed if we didn't?"

"Sir?"

"I'm not going to build another Dragonwings. When I was up there on it, I found myself wishing you were up there, and your mother with you. And I realized I couldn't have the two of them together: my family and flying. And just as I saw the hill coming at me, I realized that my family meant more to me than flying. It's enough for me now to know that I can fly."

"But what about becoming a dragon?"

"Ah, well, there's more to being a dragon than just flying," Father said. "Dragons have immense families too. It would be nice to live long enough to see my great-grandchildren. And it may be that my final test is to raise a brood of superior women and men."

"Humph," Uncle said. "Maybe that crash knocked some sense into you."

"Maybe it did." Father leaned over from his mat and picked up his tea again, moving very slowly because of his bandaged sides.

Uncle glanced at White Deer and Hand Clap. "It'll make it easier to suggest what we were thinking of, then. I think we could use a levelheaded partner."

Father shook his head. "You know what I'd do if I were a real partner instead of just a paper one like I am now." Though we had left the Company, Father had stayed a partner on paper so that he could keep me.

Uncle rubbed the tip of his nose. "Well, I wouldn't approve of your bringing your wife over here. But then I never thought I'd be friends with a demoness, nor see a man fly through the air. I will admit that I may not be right in everything." Uncle held up a warning toward us all. "But don't get the idea that I'm wrong in everything."

Father still hesitated. "Lefty has been with the Company longer."

"He's already a partner," Hand Clap said.

"They let me buy in for what I had," Lefty explained. "That was about eight hundred dollars. But I have a full thousand-dollar share."

"But I don't even have a dollar to my name," Father said.

"I'll lend you the money," Uncle said.

"A thousand dollars?" Father rubbed his chin. "At what percent?"

Uncle threw up his hands. "What kind of man do you think I am? I won't charge you any percent. That way, when I face the Judges of the Dead, I can say that I did my best to make up with you."

White Deer spread his hands. "If you can perform the miracle of flying, Uncle can perform the miracle of making a loan without any interest due on it."

"You're being too generous," Father protested.

"It's time to see that the Company can carry on without us," Uncle said. "White Deer, Hand Clap, and I won't be living forever."

I held my breath. Father turned and winked at me as if to say, "What can we do?" To Uncle, Father said, "We accept and thank you all."

I knew I spoke for both Father and me when I said, "And Uncle, we hope that you and White Deer and Hand Clap come as close to living forever as three superior men can." And then I started to translate our wonderful news for the Whitlaws.

We heard about Black Dog much later, when his coffin was shipped down to us. He had fled north to Sacramento. Poor Black Dog never even lived to spend the money he took from us. He was found in an alley with his throat slit and his wallet stolen even before he could make it to an opium den. Uncle locked himself in his room for one whole night and the next day came out as cantankerous as ever.

I think the reason Uncle had originally been so strict with Father was that he thought of Father as his spiritual son. He hoped that Windrider would be everything that Uncle had once wished Black Dog to be. And like any parent with a child, Uncle was hurt and angry when Windrider did not behave as Uncle wanted. But then, with Dragonwings, Uncle came to accept the fact that he was not always right.

Father and I moved back into the Company's new, sturdy building. It took several months for Father's broken bones to mend—and he was always to get aches in them during our cold, rainy winters. During that time we never lost contact with the Whitlaws. I had only to go next door to the Cigarmaker and use his electric talker to call them up. Every Sunday, I walked down to the *Ferry Building*. Sometimes I caught a boat over to Oakland to spend an afternoon with them. Other times I met the Whitlaws as they came over. I won't say that Miss Whitlaw and Uncle became the best of friends, but they came to like each other as much as two such different people could.

It was not until the next summer that Father got the paperwork straightened out and the proper demon officials bribed, and then he sailed for the Middle Kingdom to bring back Mother. He sailed on a Saturday, so I was able to see the Whitlaws on the very next day.

Robin and I were sitting outside on the lawn swing

behind the house where she and her aunt worked. The house was on a hillside, with the swing about thirty feet below it.

"Penny for your thoughts," Robin said.

"You'd be paying too much."

"No, really, what were you thinking?"

"I was thinking how lucky I am."

I knew there were plenty of problems still ahead of me. I had not seen my mother for something like seven years, and I knew we would have to adjust to one another. And then there were the problems of my taking on more responsibility in the Company. Tons of problems, and while I was not about to dismiss them as little ones, I was not afraid of them. I knew that I could meet them with the same courage with which Father had pursued his dream of flight and then given it up, or the same courage with which Mother had faced the long separation from us.

"I think I'm lucky too," Robin said with a sigh, and looked out at the beautiful view before us.

And then Miss Whitlaw came out of the kitchen onto the back porch. *"There's some fresh-baked cookies for anyone who's willing."*

Robin turned to me with a grin. *"I haven't had a good race in a long time."*

"Neither have I," I said. But she was already running up the hill while I was getting up. She won, of course.

Afterword

I ought to explain that when the story refers to a Tang man, he is not one of the notorious Tong men, or hatchetmen. As the story notes, the word Tang refers to the Tang dynasty, which ruled from 618 to 907 A.D., and is more properly spelled T'ang. The "Tong" of the hatchetmen is translated as brotherhood in the story, and means a hall or a court, and by extension a lodge or a fraternity.

I should also warn thoughtful readers that DRAGONWINGS is more of a historical fantasy than a factual reconstruction. I was intrigued when I first read the newspaper accounts of the young Chinese flier Fung Joe Guey. He flew in the hills of Oakland on September 22, 1909, for twenty minutes before a mishap with one propeller brought his biplane down. Not only had the ingenious Fung Joe Guey improved upon the Wrights' original design, but he had also made his own wireless sets and telephones, which he distributed among other interested Chinese. He had plans to build a new biplane of steel pipes and silk.

Did he ever build that new biplane? I do not know. Nor do I know why he built that first biplane. I do not even know where he came from or whether he had a wife and a family. Like the other Chinese who came to America, he remains a shadowy figure. Of the hundreds of thousands of Chinese who flocked to these shores we know next to nothing. They remain a dull, faceless mass: statistical fodder to be fed to the sociologists, or lifeless abstractions to be manipulated by historians. And yet these Chinese were human beings—with fears and hopes, joys and sorrows like the rest of us. In the adventures of the various members of the Company of the Peach Orchard Vow, I have tried to make some of these dry historical facts become living experiences.

At the same time, I have tried to be reasonably faithful to the period. E. Nesbit was then a new and "promising" author in England. Theodore Roosevelt was regarded as something of a wild-eyed radical by right-wingers, and he did get into office because of a presidential assassination. Similarly, I have tried to follow the facts of the Chinese-American experience when I could find them, including a description of a Chinese laundry before the earthquake.

At the same time, it has been my aim to counter various stereotypes as presented in the media. Dr. Fu Manchu and his yellow hordes, Charlie Chan and his fortune-cookie wisdom, the laundrymen and cooks of the movie and television Westerns, and the houseboys of various comedies present an image of Chinese not as they really are but as they exist in the mind of White America. I wanted to show that Chinese-Americans are human beings upon whom America has had a unique effect. I have tried to do this by seeing America through the eyes of a recently arrived Chinese boy, and by presenting the struggles of his father in following his dream.

RELATED READINGS

The Flying Machine

by Ray Bradbury

In this play, set in China 1500 years before Windrider's amazing flight, another man flies. Notice how the witnesses react to his flight.

CHARACTERS

Yuan, the Emperor

Servant

The Flying One

Time: The Past

Place: China

CURTAIN

[The Emperor (Narrator) is seen standing at C. He bows slightly, then strikes a gong nearby.]

Yuan (The Emperor). What year is this? Why—you can almost smell it, all about.

[He breathes deeply.]

The greatest year in the entire history of civilization. Of course! The year four hundred A.D., which means . . . four hundred years after the birth of some carpenter's son. . . his name . . .

[He gropes casually in his mind, cannot recall, then shrugs.]

Well, it will come to me. Anyway, the year: four hundred.

[He strikes the gong somewhat louder.]

And this . . .

[He indicates all about.]

. . . is the vast world which really is all the world known as Chan-so-Chan by the enlightened. You barbarians call us . . . China.

[He strikes the gong.]

And this . . .

[He touches himself with reverence.]

. . . is the Emperor Yuan who holds his throne by the Great Wall of China where our land is green with rain, readying itself toward future harvests, at peace, the people in our good dominion neither too happy nor too sad. Which is a remarkable and fortunate state. For if my people were too sad, the gods, curious at their weeping, might draw close and over-compensate with riches. Then, oh then! my people would be too happy! And the gods, turned about, hearing their laughter, envious of their joy, would strike them with lightning or bring the river over the banks to drown them all. No! None of that! We tread in the middle way, between laughter and tears, in the best land, in the best year . . . and now . . .

[There is a soft gong offstage and a faint tinkle of wind crystals.]

Early on the morning of the first day of the first week of the second month of the New Year, I sip my tea, I fan myself against a warm breeze . . . so . . . and then:

[The Servant *runs in, then bows.]*

Servant. Oh, Emperor, Emperor, a miracle! A miracle!

Yuan *(calmly).* Yes, the air *is* sweet this morning.

Servant *(on his knees, prostrate).* No, no, a miracle!

Yuan. And this tea is good in my mouth. Surely *that* is the miracle?

Servant. No, no, Excellency!

Yuan *(guessing).* Well, then . . . the sun has risen? A new day is upon us? The sea is blue? That now is the finest of all miracles.

Servant *(half rising to point).* Excellency, oh there, there! A man! He is flying!

Yuan *(stopping his fan).* A man? What?

Servant. I saw him in the air, a man with wings. I heard a voice call out of the vast sky and when I looked up, there it was, a strange bird in the heavens with a man in its mouth, a bird of paper and bamboo, colored like the sun and the grass—

Yuan. It is early. You have just wakened from a most lovely dream.

Servant. It is early, but I have seen what I have seen. Come. You will see it too.

Yuan. Sit down with me here. Drink some tea. It must be a strange thing, if it is true, to see a man fly. You must have time to think of it, even as I must have time to prepare myself for this sight.

[Both sit. The Emperor *pours tea for both. The* Servant *hesitates to accept this service from his lord, but the* Emperor *frowns. The* Servant *obeys, sipping the tea gingerly, once.]*

Servant *(nervously glancing beyond).* Oh, please . . . he will be gone!

Yuan. I am ready. Show me what you have seen.

[The Servant *leads the way in a great circle about the stage.* Yuan *nods to the* Servant, *then aside.]*

He leads the way. We go. We walk in gardens. We cross a small meadow of grass, over a quaint bridge, through a grove of trees, and up a tiny hill. *[He turns.]* Well?

Servant *(gazing all about, despairing, then suddenly elated).* There! Oh, there, there!

Yuan. Yes . . . there, in the sky, laughing so high that I can hardly hear him, is a man, and the man is clothed in bright papers and reeds to make wings and a beautiful bright yellow feathered tail and he is soaring all about like the largest bird in a universe of birds, like a vast and incredible new kite in a land of ancient kites.

A Voice *(from above, laughing).* I fly . . . I fly . . . Oh, I fly!

Servant *(eagerly).* Yes, yes! Oh, yes, you *do!*

[The Emperor remains strangely motionless, slowly turning to gaze here, there, and back at the sky.]

Yuan *(to himself).* Be still, O Emperor. Look at the Great Wall of China which now takes shape out of the farthest mist in the green hills, that splendid snake of stones which writhes with majesty across the entire world. See that wonderful wall which has protected a thousand villages, and ten million people for a timeless time from enemy hordes. Really see that Wall which has preserved peace for years without number. Then see our own small town, nestled to itself by a river and a road and a hill, beginning to waken. There a woman rises to cook rice. There a fisherman goes with his nets. And just beyond, a child, wrapped in the dew of early morn, rolls down a sweet meadow. *[He peers.]* Blind to all *this?*

[He glances at the sky, then back to the far people, then turns to his Servant.]

Here now . . . how many have seen this man who flies?

Servant *(waving at the sky, then stopping to look about, unsure, then sure).* Perhaps I am the only one, Excellency. Yes . . . for it is still too early. And those few who are out, their eyes are on the path where they always go.

Yuan (gazing at the sky). Good. Then call him down to me.

Servant. Ho, you there! Great Kite of dawn! Come down!

Yuan. Hist . . . that farmer in the field has lifted his head . . .

Servant [trying to yell quietly]. Come down, the Emperor wishes to see you!

Yuan. He comes. The wind brings him, gladly . . .

Servant. Oh, look, his passage writes a poem on the air!

Yuan (awestruck, but enigmatic). I wonder . . . what does it *say?*

[He and the Servant follow the flight to crystal music all about until to one side off-scene, the one who flies alights upon the grass.]

Servant. The butterfly now touches earth. And suddenly . . . a clumsy worm.

[In high good humor, The Flying One enters, proud of his feat, proud of his equipments which he brandishes, arms open, then shut, face exhilarated, turning about to look up at that sky where just a moment before he has been. His face momentarily clouds.]

Yuan. There are other kites like this?

The Flying One. Oh, none, none.

Yuan. This is the only one in all our land?

The Flying One. I swear it!

Yuan. Who else knows of this?

The Flying One. No one. Not even my wife, who would think me mad with the sun. She thought I was making only a large and strange and beautiful kite for the festival. I rose secretly in the night when she was sleeping and walked to the hills beyond, to the cliff where I gathered my courage when the morning breezes blew and the sun waited beyond the sea. Then, oh then, Excellency, I *did* become brave. I tried, I leapt out upon the air, I flew. But, as I said, the hour even now is early. People have only begun to stir. No one knows of my flight. My wife still sleeps.

Yuan. Well for her, then. Come along.

[He and The Flying One *move in a great circle.]*

Servant *(aside).* And walk we do, obedient to commands, back to the great house. Even as the sun at last dares lift its face and the land, too late for miracles, awakes. And in the fresh green smell of the garden, the Emperor, this humble servant, and the one-who-flies, stop.

[The Emperor *has clapped his hands.]*

Yuan. You! *[He points.]* On your knees!

[The Flying One *falls to his knees, bewildered.]*

You! *[He points to the* Servant.*]* Call the Executioner!

[The Servant *starts off, then turns around, startled.]*

Servant. But I, Your Excellency, *I* am the Executioner!

Yuan. Yes, yes. How strange we *both* forgot. How many years has it been since you . . . No matter. Bring the sword.

Servant. The sword! *[He exits.]*

The Flying One. The sword? What? Why?

[Face bowed, eyes shut, his shoulders move in silent weeping.]

[The Servant returns with a sword. He sees The Flying One kneeling and comments on what he sees.]

Servant. He weeps. And hear! How his sadness makes the beautiful wings . . . *whisper!*

The Flying One. What, what have I done?

Yuan. Can it be true you do not know? You build and know not what you build? Create and know not the child of your creation? *[He gazes close at* The Flying One.*]* Yes. Your face is as clear as mountain water. There is no evil there. And yet . . . *[He nods at the* Servant. *The* Servant *claps on his Executioner's dark mask.]*

The Flying One. Wait! I don't understand!

Yuan *[holding up a hand quietly]*. Wait indeed. For then I must explain. Here on this table, see? A machine that I myself have dreamt to being. Here now, from about my neck, I take a golden key. I fit this key to the tiny delicate machine. I wind it up. Thus. Then, stand back, and set its cogs in motion . . . so.

[Faint crystal music, a sound of birds and fountains. The Servant *forgets his sword,* The Flying One *his possible death. Both look to the device, seen if we wish; unseen if we wish the* Emperor *to wind it up in pantomime.]*

The Flying One *(stunned)*. What . . . machine is *this?*

Yuan. A toy garden wrought from metal and inlaid with jewels. A green forest of bronze and brass and iron one can hold in these two hands. Its spring wound and set to move, birds, do you see them? sing in tiny metal trees, wolves walk through miniature forests and tiny people run forth in sun and shadow. There! they fan themselves with miniature jade fans. And there! listen to the tiny emerald birds. And there! stand by impossibly small but bright and leaping founts of water.

The Flying One *(gazing, half-risen)*. Beautiful.

Yuan. Is it not? So if you asked me: what have I done here? I could answer well. I have made birds sing. I have made forests murmur. I have set people to walking in this woodland glade, shadowed by leaves, moved by song. *That* is what I have done.

The Flying One *(remembering his position, dropping back to one knee)*. But, O Emperor, I have done a similar thing! I have found beauty. I have flown on the morning wind. I have looked down on all the sleeping houses and gardens. I have smelled the sea and even seen it, beyond the hills, from my high place. And I have soared like a bird. Oh, I cannot tell how beautiful it is up there, in the sky, with the wind suspending and bearing me here like a feather, there like a fan, and away like my son's first festival kite . . . and the way the very *stuff* of the sky smells on such a morning, and how free one feels! That is beautiful, Emperor, that is beautiful, *too!*

Yuan *(nodding slowly with understanding)*. Yes. I believe. For I felt my heart move with you in the air and I wondered, oh what must it be like? How must it seem? How do the distant pools look from high above? And how my gardens and my servants should they come upon the road? Like toys to be scattered by the beating of your wings! And the distant towns in the early morning mists; the look of *them!* Lovely. Lovely.

The Flying One *(seizing on the* Emperor's *comprehension).* Yes. Yes. You understand. So spare me!

Yuan. There are times when one must lose a little beauty if one is to keep what little beauty one already has. I do not fear you.

The Flying One. What man?

Yuan. Another man who seeing you build a bright contraption of papers and bamboo will go build for himself a similar device. But this other man, nameless now, faceless now, will turn at last to show his evil glance and evil heart. Then; beauty vanishes. *That* man I fear.

The Flying One. Why?

Yuan. Look there, to the north and west, what do you see?

The Flying One. The Great Wall of China.

Yuan. The Great Wall of China, which does what?

The Flying One. Why . . . which protects us from the invasions of the Mongol hordes.

Yuan. And for how many years has the Great Wall shielded us?

The Flying One. A thousand years!

Yuan. A thousand years. Then listen further, you with your bright wings. I see this other man with an evil heart borrowing or stealing your wings. I see him flying in the air. And I see him drop huge stones upon that Great Wall of China. Huge stones upon the Great Wall . . .

[There is silence. The impact of the words is enough. The Emperor *speaks no more. The weight of what he has said sinks* The Flying One *to his knees. He bows his head, eyes shut.]*

The Flying One *(with sad understanding).* Yes . . . I *see . . .* yes. *[After a beat, the* Emperor *speaks sharply, quickly.]*

Yuan. Off with his head. Burn the wings and this man's body and bury their ashes together, in an unmarked grave. Hold your tongue. It was all a dream, a most sorrowful and beautiful dream. Go among all my people in the town. Listen. If you find one who, rising early, saw the strange bird in the sky, kill him. I shall let you live as long as you stay silent.

Servant. You are merciful, Emperor.

[The Emperor *nods quickly. The* Servant *seizes* The Flying One *to his feet and runs him out, the sharp sword ready. The* Emperor *stares off-scene as there is a great whistling sound, a cry, then an exhaled grunt.]*

Yuan *[in spite of himself, shocked].* Merciful! *[A beat, looking down.]* Merciful? No. Only very much bewildered and afraid. What is the life of that one poor man against those of a million others I must protect? I must take solace from that thought. There . . . the fire burns. The bright paper wings go up in flame. *[We see the pattern of smoke upon a scrim of sky to one side.]* The unmarked grave is dug where Time, some little while, must sleep to wake again some other year. Here, take this key again. Wind up the beautiful miniature machineries of jeweled garden. There. *[He winds.]* And look across the land to the Great Wall still one piece, the green fields, the protected towns, the rivers and streams. While here . . . *[He* *sighs, then looks at the toy clasped in his hands.]* . . . The tiny garden whirs its hidden and delicate cogs and wheels no larger than this fingernail. Ah . . . tiny people walk in forests, tiny foxes lope through sun-dappled glades in beautiful shining pelts. Among the microscopic trees fly tiny bits of high song and bright blue and yellow color, soaring, climbing, circling in this small hand-clasped sky I hold and keep. Oh, oh, look at the birds! *[He has been peering at the exquisite machine in his hands all this while. At the last, he raises his gaze to the real sky above.]* Look at the birds! *[He shuts his eyes to see them fly within his mind, in toneless despair.]* Look at the birds . . .

CURTAIN

Crazy Boys

by Beverly McLoughland

Were they crazy or were they Wright?

Watching buzzards,
Flying kites,
Lazy, crazy boys
The Wrights. They

5   Tried to fly
Just like a bird
Foolish dreamers
Strange. Absurd. We

10 Scoffed and scorned
Their dreams of flight
But we were wrong
And they were Wright.

The Skydivers

by Joseph Colin Murphey

How might Windrider feel about this poem?

This is a fervent time
    for flying.
        Do not foul
        my fall in a fit
5   of wing-waggling!
    Hold
    steady
    as
    we
10   touch.
    The
    force
    of
    flight
15   tears
    away
    all
    sham.
    Enter
20   upon
    the
    wind's
    fingers.
    H
25   o
    o
    o
    o
    l
30   d
    !
    m
    e
    e
35   e
    e
    e
    !

'The Chinese Must Go'

by Bernard A. Weisberger

Xenophobia is the hatred and fear of foreigners. Just as the Chinese experienced the effects of xenophobia, so do immigrants today.

One splendid morning during a recent West Coast vacation, I was turning the pages of a San Francisco newspaper over my coffee when I came upon a headline that clouded my cheerful mood: GERMAN POLL FINDS SENTIMENT AGAINST FOREIGNERS RUNS DEEP. According to the story below it, one-quarter of a group of Germans polled in a survey agreed entirely or partly with the slogan "Germany for the Germans," which right-wing extremists had been chanting during several weeks of rampages against foreign refugees. Included in the atrocities were the rock-throwing attacks on refugee shelters and the torching of foreigners' homes. "Shades of the 1930s," I thought with the automatic shudder that any possible neo-Nazi activity sends through me—in Germany or anywhere else.

Then I thought a bit longer. Something tickled my memory, and it flashed a new message: "Shades of the 1870s too. And not in Europe but in San Francisco, California!" I remembered that San Francisco had been seized, in 1877, by a violent spasm of antiforeign, specifically anti-Chinese, feeling that broke into murderous riots against innocents of the "wrong" ancestry. The fever started among working-class whites, but before it ran its full course, it infected the governments of both California and the United States, with long-lasting results.

Please understand that I have no intention of drawing farfetched comparisons, or of calling Americans of the 1870s neo-Nazis—quite the contrary. Nor do I aim to exonerate the 1990s neo-Nazis by trite reminders that they are not the first, last, or only haters to sully history's pages with brutality. Still, one of the best things about good history is its power to reduce national arrogance and to promote reflection and caution. So this story needs telling.

Xenophobia wasn't new in the United States a century and a quarter ago. A strong nativist movement before the Civil War had been responsible for discrimination and occasional violence against foreign-born Catholics. In the 1850s the Protestant crusade went political in the shape of the American (or "Know-Nothing") party and scored some short-term gains. But California's nativism in 1877 was especially sharp after four years of a bitter depression that had begun in 1873. (Economic pain will do that every time; the 1992 wave of German antiforeignism is strongest in formerly Communist East Germany, where unemployment is high and living standards low.)

America in 1877 was hurting all over, but as is often the case, the situation was special in California, particularly in San Francisco. It was less than thirty years since the gold rush had filled the city with brazen fortune seekers. The giddiness of their expectations was now offset by brutal reality, and most of them were facing the fact that they would spend their lives in a postboom economy. Gold and silver production was down, and unemployment now hovered around 20 percent. Where land had been plentiful, the best acreage was being concentrated into great estates.

Where San Francisco grocers had made fortunes selling infrequent shiploads of coveted goods, they now faced tough competition in a national market created by the newly completed transcontinental railroad line. And that same railroad, once hailed as the salvation of California, had become a monster monopoly that was charged with gouging the state's shippers and buying exemption from the law by bribing and lobbying.

The Big Four who built and owned the Southern Pacific Railroad—Mark Hopkins, Charles Crocker, Collis P. Huntington, and Leland Stanford—typified the widening social chasm. Basically storekeepers who had struck it rich by their timely investment in the rails, they and other new millionaires built, on San Francisco's Nob Hill, gingerbread mansions tended by liveried servants. Thus, the social cast of San Francisco included a restless down-at-the-heels population, a class of power-flaunting neoaristocrats, a supervillain in the shape of a railroad monopoly— and, finally, a set of scapegoats in the Chinese.

There were between twelve thousand and twenty-two thousand of them in the city, all recent immigrants and visibly, achingly different in their Manchu pigtails and their "bizarre" customs. They had been run out of the mining camps by discriminatory state laws and vigilante violence and settled in the cities to cook and wash for the Anglo-Saxons. Then the Big Four had discovered that they made wonderful railroad-construction workers—patient, diligent, and, above all, vulnerable and therefore cheap. Crocker imported thousands of them. So did other employers through wholesale contracts with Chinese labor agents. The Chinese composed perhaps only 15 percent of the San Francisco labor force, but they were blamed and hated by apparently every unemployed or underemployed white San Franciscan.

On July 23, 1877, the trigger on violence was pulled by news from the East. Between July 14 and 26 striking rail workers had clashed with militia in Pittsburgh, Baltimore, Chicago, and Martinsburg, West Virginia. At least seventy people had been murdered in the tumult. A meeting in support of the strikers was called in an empty downtown sandlot in San Francisco by sympathizers associated with the ten-year-old Marxist International Association of Workingmen. The crowd shouted its approval of anticapitalist resolutions. Then, inevitably, someone cried, "On to Chinatown," and the mob boiled out to look for victims. Twenty laundries were burned that night. On the next, there was an attack on a woolen mill employing many Chinese workers. At that the city fathers, alarmed about threats to property, formed a Committee of Safety and called out the militia. On the third night the rioters attacked the docks of the Pacific Steamship Company and set fire to a lumberyard. Police charged their ranks; four rioters were killed and fourteen wounded. That was the end of the collective violence.

But not of the anti-Chinese revolt. Two months later the crowd found a leader in a thirty-year-old Irish-born small businessman named Denis Kearney. Self-made and self-educated, Kearney was the guiding spirit in creating a new organization, the Working-men's Party of California (WPC). Night after night he held forth to sandlot crowds in speeches full of political brimstone, like his pronouncement that "the dignity of labor must be sustained, even if we have to kill every wretch that opposes it." He frightened the city fathers enough to have him arrested in November, but since his threats were always vaguely conditional rather than immediate, he was acquitted. Actually, he mainly urged his audiences to vote for delegates to a forthcoming state constitutional convention that he hoped would empower "the people" by tightly regulating corporations and their lobbyists and subsidies. But his most powerful attention-getter was a demand for an end to the immigration and hiring of Chinese. "We intend to try and vote the Chinaman out, to frighten him out, and if this won't do, to kill him out. . . . The heathen slaves must leave this coast." He boiled it down to a sledgehammer four-word cry: "The Chinese must go!"

Kearney touched on worker anxieties with his hints of a scheme by the rich to bring feudalism to the United States through the replacement of American workingmen with "coolies" who would neither expect nor receive a living wage or democratic rights.

He enjoyed fleeting political success. The Workingmen's Party of California won many local and state offices in 1878 and named fifty-two delegates to the convention, which did include some of their proposals in the new Constitution of 1879. But the antibusiness strictures were gradually eviscerated by the courts and by lack of implementation, and the WPC faded away, though Kearney himself lived on until 1907. Kearney's legislative influence was brief, but the evil that he did to the Chinese lived after him.

That was because "The Chinese must go" had more than local impact. It struck powerful echoes in a time of social Darwinist racism. The Chinese were almost universally disdained by the "advanced" Americans. The newspaper baron James Gordon Bennett discouraged their immigration with the comment that only "on the Caucasian element can we hope to build up such an empire as the world has never seen." Other opinion makers, lumping all classes and conditions of Chinese together, labeled them "ignorant of civilized life" or "listless, stagnant [and] unprogressive." In the popular image they were criminals, gamblers, prostitutes, and opium smokers. In Far Western towns Chinese storekeepers were often beaten and robbed by drunken miners and cowboys, or at a minimum tormented by teen-age hoodlums. And in 1885 twenty-eight Chinese were massacred in Rock Springs, Wyoming.

Therefore, legal exclusion was easily enacted. California in 1880 virtually shut the door on the importation and use of Chinese labor. The Congress of the United States followed suit with the Exclusion Act of 1882, barring all Chinese immigration for ten years. Renewed and renewed, the exclusion policy remained in force until World War II, when it began to be modified gradually until it was finally dropped, after eighty-six years, in a 1968 overhaul of immigration legislation.

It would be possible and pleasant to conclude this column on an upbeat note. Anti-Asian prejudice in the United States is only a glimmer of its former self, and the Chinese are even considered a "model minority," held up for others' emulation. That is certainly a credit to American pluralism. But the virus of xenophobia is never really extinguished in any multiethnic body politic. It merely becomes temporarily inactive. And as for racism—enough said. Human beings have an inextinguishable capacity to be cruel to one another, particularly in groups. It takes constant self-reminders of how bad things can get to keep alive the energy to make them better.

Ginger for the Heart

by Paul Yee

*Nearly all the Chinese immigrants to North
America in the early years of the 20th
century could tell tales of loved ones left
behind. Here is one such story.*

The buildings of Chinatown are stoutly constructed
of brick, and while some are broad and others thin,
they rise no higher than four solid storeys. Many
contain stained-glass windows decorated with flower
and diamond patterns, and others boast balconies
with fancy wrought-iron railings.

Only one building stands above the rest. Its
turret-like tower is visible even from the harbor,
because the cone-shaped roof is made of copper.

In the early days, Chang the merchant tailor
owned this building. He used the main floor for his
store and rented out the others. But he kept the
tower room for his own use, for the sun filled it with
light. This was the room where his wife and daughter
worked.

His daughter's name was Yenna, and her beauty
was beyond compare. She had ivory skin, sparkling
eyes, and her hair hung long and silken, shining like
polished ebony. All day long she and her mother sat
by the tower window and sewed with silver needles
and silken threads. They sang songs while they
worked, and their voices rose in wondrous
harmonies.

In all Chinatown, the craftsmanship of Yenna and
her mother was considered the finest. Search as they
might, customers could not discern where holes had

once pierced their shirts. Buttonholes never stretched out of shape, and seams were all but invisible.

One day, a young man came into the store laden with garments for mending. His shoulders were broad and strong, yet his eyes were soft and caring. Many times he came, and many times he saw Yenna. For hours he would sit and watch her work. They fell deeply in love, though few words were spoken between them.

Spring came and boats bound for the northern gold fields began to sail again. It was time for the young man to go. He had borrowed money to pay his way over to the New World, and now he had to repay his debts. Onto his back he threw his blankets and tools, food and warm jackets. Then he set off with miners from around the world, clutching gold pans and shovels.

Yenna had little to give him in farewell. All she found in the kitchen was a ginger root as large as her hand. As she stroked its brown knobs and bumpy eyes, she whispered to him, "This will warm you in the cold weather. I will wait for you, but, like this piece of ginger, I, too, will age and grow dry." Then she pressed her lips to the ginger, and turned away.

"I will come back," the young man said. "The fire burning for you in my heart can never be extinguished."

Thereafter, Yenna lit a lamp at every nightfall and set it in the tower window. Rains lashed against the glass, snow piled low along the ledge, and ocean winds rattled the frame. But the flame did not waver, even though the young man never sent letters. Yenna did not weep uselessly, but continued to sew and sing with her mother.

There were few unmarried women in Chinatown, and many men came to seek Yenna's hand in marriage. Rich gold miners and sons of successful merchants bowed before her, but she always looked away. They gave her grand gifts, but still she shook her head, until finally the men grew weary and called her crazy. In China, parents arranged all marriages, and daughters became the property of their husbands. But Chang the merchant tailor treasured his daughter's happiness and let her be.

One winter, an epidemic ravaged the city. When it was over, Chang had lost his wife and his eyesight. Yenna led him up to the tower where he could feel the sun and drifting clouds move across his face. She began to sew again, and while she sewed, she sang for her father. The lamp continued to burn steadily at the tower window as she worked. With twice the amount of work to do, she labored long after dusk. She fed the flame more oil and sent her needle skimming through the heavy fabrics. Nimbly her fingers braided shiny cords and coiled them into butterfly buttons. And when the wick sputtered into light each evening, Yenna's heart soared momentarily into her love's memories. Nights passed into weeks, months turned into years, and four years quickly flew by.

One day a dusty traveler came into the store and flung a bundle of ragged clothes onto the counter. Yenna shook out the first shirt, and out rolled a ginger root. Taking it into her hand, she saw that pieces had been nibbled off, but the core of the root was still firm and fragrant.

She looked up. There stood the man she had promised to wait for. His eyes appeared older and wiser.

"Your gift saved my life several times," he said. "The fire of the ginger is powerful indeed."

"Why is the ginger root still firm and heavy?" she

wondered. "Should it not have dried and withered?"

"I kept it close to my heart and my sweat coated it. In lonely moments, my tears soaked it." His calloused hands reached out for her. "Your face has not changed."

"Nor has my heart," she replied. "I have kept a lamp burning all these years."

"So I have heard," he smiled. "Will you come away with me now? It has taken many years to gather enough gold to buy a farm. I have built you a house on my land."

For the first time since his departure, tears cascaded down Yenna's face. She shook her head. "I cannot leave. My father needs me."

"Please come with me," the young man pleaded. "You will be very happy, I promise."

Yenna swept the wetness from her cheeks. "Stay with me and work this store instead," she implored.

The young man stiffened and stated proudly, "A man does not live in his wife's house." And the eyes that she remembered so well gleamed with determination.

"But this is a new land," she cried. "Must we forever follow the old ways?"

She reached out for him, but he brushed her away. With a curse, he hurled the ginger root into the fireplace. As the flames leapt up, Yenna's eyes blurred. The young man clenched and unclenched his fists in anger. They stood like stone.

At last the man turned to leave, but suddenly he knelt at the fireplace. Yenna saw him reach in with the tongs and pull something out of the flames.

"Look!" he whispered in amazement. "The ginger refuses to be burnt! The flames cannot touch it!"

Yenna looked and saw black burn marks charring the root, but when she took it in her hand, she found it still firm and moist. She held it to her nose, and found the fragrant sharpness still there.

The couple embraced and swore to stay together. They were married at a lavish banquet attended by all of Chinatown. There, the father passed his fingers over his son-in-law's face and nodded in satisfaction.

Shortly after, the merchant Chang died, and the young couple moved away. Yenna sold the business and locked up the tower room. But on nights when boats pull in from far away, they say a flicker of light can still be seen in that high window. And Chinese women are reminded that ginger is one of their best friends.

The Story of an Eyewitness

by Jack London

London, author of The Call of The Wild *and other adventure novels, writes a hair-raising description of the San Francisco earthquake of 1906. Compare his eyewitness report with Yep's fictional account.*

The earthquake shook down in San Francisco hundreds of thousands of dollars' worth of walls and chimneys. But the conflagration that followed burned up hundreds of millions of dollars' worth of property. There is no estimating within hundreds of millions the actual damage wrought. Not in history has a modern imperial city been so completely destroyed. San Francisco is gone. Nothing remains of it but memories and a fringe of dwelling houses on its outskirts. Its industrial section is wiped out. Its business section is wiped out. Its social and residential section is wiped out. The factories and warehouses, the great stores and newspaper buildings, the hotels and the palaces of the nabobs, are all gone. Remains only the fringe of dwelling houses on the outskirts of what was once San Francisco.

Within an hour after the earthquake shock, the smoke of San Francisco's burning was a lurid tower visible a hundred miles away. And for three days and nights this lurid tower swayed in the sky, reddening the sun, darkening the day, and filling the land with smoke.

On Wednesday morning at a quarter past five came

the earthquake. A minute later the flames were leaping upward. In a dozen different quarters south of Market Street, in the working-class ghetto, and in the factories, fires started. There was no opposing the flames. There was no organization, no communication. All the cunning adjustments of a twentieth-century city had been smashed by the earthquake. The streets were humped into ridges and depressions, and piled with the debris of fallen walls. The steel rails were twisted into perpendicular and horizontal angles. The telephone and telegraph systems were disrupted. And the great water mains had burst. All the shrewd contrivances and safeguards of man had been thrown out of gear by thirty seconds twitching of the earthcrust.

By Wednesday afternoon, inside of twelve hours, half the heart of the city was gone. At that time, I watched the vast conflagration from out on the bay. It was dead calm. Not a flicker of wind stirred. Yet from every side wind was pouring in upon the city. East, west, north, and south, strong winds were blowing upon the doomed city. The heated air rising made an enormous suck. Thus did the fire of itself build its own colossal chimney through the atmosphere. Day and night this dead calm continued, and yet, near to the flames, the wind was often half a gale, so mighty was the suck.

Wednesday night saw the destruction of the very heart of the city. Dynamite was lavishly used, and many of San Francisco's proudest structures were crumbled by man himself into ruins, but there was no withstanding the onrush of the flames. Time and again successful stands were made by the firefighters, and every time the flames flanked around on either side, or came up from the rear, and turned to defeat the hard-won victory.

An enumeration of the buildings destroyed would

be a directory of San Francisco. An enumeration of the buildings undestroyed would be a line and several addresses. An enumeration of the deeds of heroism would stock a library and bankrupt the Carnegie Medal Fund. An enumeration of the dead—will never be made. All vestiges of them were destroyed by the flames. The number of the victims of the earthquake will never be known. South of Market Street, where the loss of life was particularly heavy, was the first to catch fire.

Remarkable as it may seem, Wednesday night, while the whole city crashed and roared into ruin, was a quiet night. There were no crowds. There was no shouting and yelling. There was no hysteria, no disorder. I passed Wednesday night in the path of the advancing flames, and in all those terrible hours I saw not one woman who wept, not one man who was excited, not one person who was in the slightest degree panic-stricken.

Before the flames, throughout the night, fled tens of thousands of homeless ones. Some were wrapped in blankets. Others carried bundles of bedding and dear household treasures. Sometimes a whole family was harnessed to a carriage or delivery wagon that was weighted down with their possessions. Baby buggies, toy wagons, and go-carts were used as trucks, while every other person was dragging a trunk. Yet everybody was gracious. The most perfect courtesy obtained. Never, in all San Francisco's history, were her people so kind and courteous as on this night of terror.

All night these tens of thousands fled before the flames. Many of them, the poor people from the labor ghetto, had fled all day as well. They had left their homes burdened with possessions. Now and again they lightened up, flinging out upon the street clothing and treasures they had dragged for miles.

They held on longest to their trunks, and over these trunks many a strong man broke his heart that night. The hills of San Francisco are steep, and up these hills, mile after mile, were the trunks dragged. Everywhere were trunks, with across them lying their exhausted owners, men and women. Before the march of the flames were flung picket lines of soldiers. And a block at a time, as the flames advanced, these pickets retreated. One of their tasks was to keep the trunk pullers moving. The exhausted creatures, stirred on by the menace of bayonets, would arise and struggle up the steep pavements, pausing from weakness every five or ten feet.

Often, after surmounting a heartbreaking hill, they would find another wall of flame advancing upon them at right angles and be compelled to change anew the line of their retreat. In the end, completely played out, after toiling for a dozen hours like giants, thousands of them were compelled to abandon their trunks. Here the shopkeepers and soft members of the middle class were at a disadvantage. But the workingmen dug holes in vacant lots and backyards and buried their trunks.

At nine o'clock Wednesday evening I walked down through the very heart of the city. I walked through miles and miles of magnificent buildings and towering skyscrapers. Here was no fire. All was in perfect order. The police patrolled the streets. Every building had its watchman at the door. And yet it was doomed, all of it. There was no water. The dynamite was giving out. And at right angles two different conflagrations were sweeping down upon it.

At one o'clock in the morning I walked down through the same section. Everything still stood intact. There was no fire. And yet there was a change. A rain of ashes was falling. The watchmen at the doors were gone. The police had been withdrawn. There were no firemen, no fire engines, no men fighting with dynamite. The district had been absolutely abandoned. I stood at the corner of Kearney and Market, in the very innermost heart of San Francisco. Kearney Street was deserted. Half a dozen blocks away it was burning on both sides. The street was a wall of flame. And against this wall of flame, silhouetted sharply, were two United States cavalrymen sitting their horses, calmly watching. That was all. Not another person was in sight. In the intact heart of the city two troopers sat their horses and watched.

Surrender was complete. There was no water. The sewers had long since been pumped dry. There was no dynamite. Another fire had broken out further uptown, and now from three sides conflagrations were sweeping down. The fourth side had been burned earlier in the day. In that direction stood the tottering walls of the Examiner building, the burned-out Call building, the smoldering ruins of the Grand Hotel, and the gutted, devastated, dynamited Palace Hotel.

The following will illustrate the sweep of the flames and the inability of men to calculate their spread. At eight o'clock Wednesday evening I passed through Union Square. It was packed with refugees. Thousands of them had gone to bed on the grass. Government tents had been set up, supper was being cooked, and the refugees were lined up for free meals.

At half past one in the morning three sides of Union Square were in flames. The fourth side, where stood the great St. Francis Hotel, was still holding out. An hour later, ignited from top and sides, the St. Francis was flaming heavenward. Union Square, heaped high with mountains of trunks, was deserted. Troops, refugees, and all had retreated.

It was at Union Square that I saw a man offering a thousand dollars for a team of horses. He was in charge of a truck piled high with trunks from some hotel. It had been hauled here into what was considered safety, and the horses had been taken out. The flames were on three sides of the Square, and there were no horses.

Also, at this time, standing beside the truck, I urged a man to seek safety in flight. He was all but hemmed in by several conflagrations. He was an old man and he was on crutches. Said he, "Today is my birthday. Last night I was worth thirty thousand dollars. I bought five bottles of wine, some delicate fish, and other things for my birthday dinner. I have had no dinner, and all I own are these crutches."

I convinced him of his danger and started him limping on his way. An hour later, from a distance, I saw the truckload of trunks burning merrily in the middle of the street.

On Thursday morning, at a quarter past five, just twenty-four hours after the earthquake, I sat on the steps of a small residence on Nob Hill. With me sat Japanese, Italians, Chinese, and Negroes—a bit of the cosmopolitan flotsam of the wreck of the city. All about were the palaces of the nabob pioneers of Forty-nine. To the east and south, at right angles, were advancing two mighty walls of flame.

I went inside with the owner of the house on the steps of which I sat. He was cool and cheerful and hospitable. "Yesterday morning," he said, "I was worth six hundred thousand dollars. This morning this house is all I have left. It will go in fifteen minutes." He pointed to a large cabinet. "That is my wife's collection of china. This rug upon which we stand is a present. It cost fifteen hundred dollars. Try that piano. Listen to its tone. There are few like it. There are no horses. The flames will be here in fifteen minutes."

Outside, the old Mark Hopkins residence, a palace, was just catching fire. The troops were falling back and driving the refugees before them. From every side came the roaring of flames, the crashing of walls, and the detonations of dynamite.

I passed out of the house. Day was trying to dawn through the smoke-pall. A sickly light was creeping over the face of things. Once only the sun broke through the smoke-pall, blood-red, and showing a quarter its usual size. The smoke-pall itself, viewed from beneath, was a rose color that pulsed and fluttered with lavender shades. Then it turned to mauve and yellow and dun. There was no sun. And so dawned the second day on stricken San Francisco.

An hour later I was creeping past the shattered dome of the City Hall. Than it, there was no better exhibit of the destructive forces of the earthquake. Most of the stone had been shaken from the great dome, leaving standing the naked framework of steel. Market Street was piled high with the wreckage, and across the wreckage lay the overthrown pillars of the City Hall shattered into short crosswise sections.

This section of the city, with the exception of the Mint and the Post Office, was already a waste of smoking ruins. Here and there through the smoke, creeping warily under the shadows of tottering walls, emerged occasional men and women. It was like the meeting of the handful of survivors after the day of the end of the world.

On Mission Street lay a dozen steers, in a neat row stretching across the street, just as they had been struck down by the flying ruins of the earthquake. The fire had passed through afterward and roasted them.

The human dead had been carried away before the fire came. At another place on Mission Street I saw a milk wagon. A steel telegraph pole had smashed down sheer through the driver's seat and crushed the front wheels. The milk cans lay scattered around. All day Thursday and all Thursday night, all day Friday and Friday night, the flames still raged.

Friday night saw the flames finally conquered, though not until Russian Hill and Telegraph Hill had been swept and three quarters of a mile of wharves and docks had been licked up.

The great stand of the firefighters was made Thursday night on Van Ness Avenue. Had they failed here, the comparatively few remaining houses of the city would have been swept. Here were the magnificent residences of the second generation of San Francisco nabobs, and these, in a solid zone, were dynamited down across the path of the fire. Here and there the flames leaped the zone, but these fires were beaten out, principally by the use of wet blankets and rugs.

San Francisco, at the present time, is like the crater of a volcano, around which are camped tens of thousands of refugees. At the Presidio alone are at least twenty thousand. All the surrounding cities and towns are jammed with the homeless ones, where they are being cared for by relief committees. The refugees were carried free by the railroads to any point they wished to go, and it is estimated that over one hundred thousand people have left the peninsula on which San Francisco stood. The government has the situation in hand, and, thanks to the immediate relief given by the whole United States, there is not the slightest possibility of a famine. The bankers and businessmen have already set about making preparations to rebuild San Francisco.